PRINTMAKING WITH MONOTYPE

PRINTMAKING WITH

CHILTON COMPANY · BOOK DIVISION

PHILADELPHIA & NEW YORK *Publishers*

MONOTYPE

By HENRY RASMUSEN

To PAM

without whom . . .

ACKNOWLEDGMENTS

After experimenting for some time with transfer methods and becoming aware of the multitude of possibilities here for the creative artist, the author was persuaded to do something about it by compiling and writing such a book as this so that others might share his enthusiasm.

Research showed that there had been numerous short articles printed in books, art and printmaking journals, but no full-length book ever had been published on the subject. So we can claim, modestly or otherwise, that *Printmaking with Monotype* is a "first."

Questionnaires were sent out to a large number of artists who had worked with monotype or similar processes, and the generous response was most gratifying. In this regard, thanks are due to nearly all of the contemporary artists mentioned in the text or represented in the illustrations, for their kind co-operation and assistance.

While there were many duplications in the answers, making it impossible in some cases to credit any particular contributor for certain ideas or processes, a number of original ones were submitted.

The many museums, galleries, and libraries that were helpful in submitting names of monotypists and bibliographical sources are too numerous to mention here, for such a list would include most of those of any importance in this country and several abroad. The author is grateful for their assistance in research.

Appreciation is also due to the many persons and institutions granting permission to reproduce the works used as illustrations in the book.

CONTENTS

ACKNOWLEDGMENTS, vi

THE MONOTYPE · WHAT AND WHY, 1

HISTORY OF THE MONOTYPE, 9

MATERIALS AND EQUIPMENT, 93
    PLATES, 95
    MEDIA, 96
    THINNERS · BINDERS · DRIERS, 97
    TOOLS, 99
    PRESSES, 99
    PAPERS, 101

MONOTYPE AND RELATED TECHNIQUES, 103
    SUBTRACTIVE METHOD, 105
    ADDITIVE METHOD, 115
    THIN PIGMENT METHOD, 123
    OVERLAY PRINTING, 142
    CYLINDER TRANSFER, 145
    WOODBLOCK TRANSFER, 154
    BLOCKPRINT MONOTYPE, 155
    ETCHING MONOTYPE, 158
    PHOTOGRAPH MONOTYPE, 161
    CRAYON MONOTYPE, 162
    TRANSFER DRAWINGS, 172
    WATERCOLOR MONOTYPE, 174
    MIXED MEDIA, 179
    CONCLUSION, 179

BIBLIOGRAPHY, 180

INDEX, 183

THE MONOTYPE · WHAT AND WHY

On the surface it would seem like a simple thing to describe exactly what a monotype or monoprint is. After a good deal of study on the subject, the author is tempted to paraphrase Benedetto Croce's definition of art—"Art is what everybody knows it is," and say that *a monotype can be almost anything*.

If given the usual definition that a monotype is made by painting a design or picture on a piece of glass, metal, or similar surface and transferring it to paper or other material, the etcher may answer, "Then I must be a monotypist, for I use such transfer methods." The blockprint maker and even certain painters using transfer techniques in oils, enamels, or watercolors might say the same thing.

One can narrow the definition down to some extent by analyzing the word "monotype," which derives from the word, *mono,* meaning *single,* or *one of its kind,* and the word, *type,* meaning,

impressed form or print, the two together meaning, *single impression*.

This would eliminate etchings and blockprints produced in more than one like impression, and of course the goal of most printmakers other than monotypists is to achieve maximum production. However, there is still the fact that in some etching processes, such as the aquatint, there is sometimes considerable difference between one print and another. This variation is even greater in the proofs pulled from different states in the development of an etching. There is also some variation between each blockprint that is hand colored before each impression. These forms could come within the meaning of the word, "monotype," as previously stated —yet we still must arrive at a closer definition than this.

A traditional description is that a monotype is a *planographic print form leaving no residual plate*. To distin-

3

guish it from other forms, it is ordinarily printed from a plate that has no incised lines on it.

There are a number of artists using transfer techniques such as applying pigment to various cutout shapes of wood, metal, or cardboard, and impressing these patterns onto paper, canvas, or other support, building up a single picture in gradual steps. The completed work is a unique impression done by a transfer method, yet it could hardly be called a true monotype.

One who considers himself a monotypist would point out that, according to the accepted tradition, the picture on the glass or metal plate should be completed before transferring it to paper or some other surface. This requirement would eliminate quite a large group of printmakers and painters, including those who use two or more applications or overlays to produce a particular print.

It can be seen at this point that to arrive at a definition of a true monotype, the field becomes a very narrow one. Our aim is not to limit it, but rather to widen it, but in order to arrive at a working definition of the subject it is necessary to narrow it down.

So now we have this as a definition: *A monotype is a unique, printed impression produced by painting a picture or design on a plain surface, such as glass or metal, and transferring it to another surface, such as paper or cardboard.*

According to this, there are four points of distinction between a monotype and other kinds of prints: (*a*) the completion of painting first, (*b*) on a plain (unincised) surface, (*c*) the transference to another surface, and (*d*) its singularity. The more exactly any finished print comes to fulfilling these requirements, the nearer it approaches to being a true monotype.

This is about as near as this writer can come to a definition of the subject, and he will leave the question as to where one medium begins and another leaves off for others to decide. When is a blockprint a monotype, or when is a monotype a painting, are questions sometimes impossible to answer.

The fact is that in these days of free experimentation with forms and techniques, it is quite often impossible to distinguish one medium from another, even in such formerly distinct fields as painting, sculpture, and architecture.

Actually the monotype is a process, a method, or a technique which can be useful and rewarding in its own right, or in any of the fields of printmaking or painting. The purpose of this book is to outline some of the possibilities of the process, both in its relatively pure state and in combination with other methods.

When it is learned that only a single impression can be obtained from each design, the novice may wonder what the advantages are in using the method. If one is not interested in multiple

4

duplication, as in etching or blockprinting, why go to the bother of painting on one surface and transferring it to another—why not just paint the design directly onto the paper in the first place?

The most important answer is that, as can be seen better in an original than in a printed reproduction, by transferring the design from one surface to another, certain effects can be produced that can be duplicated in no other way, effects which are subtle, varied, and beautiful.

There is usually no difficulty in obtaining showings of monotypes in solo exhibits, nor in all-monotype showings, for museum and gallery directors find the unique character of the medium attractive to the viewing public.

Sometimes, however, there is difficulty in getting monotypes accepted in general print exhibitions, some printmakers and museum directors being prejudiced against the monotype as a pure print medium.

In the field of art, the monotype is admittedly a strange bird. As one print curator remarked to the author, "It is neither fish nor fowl." Because of its odd character, being neither printmaking nor painting in the ordinary sense, but a child of both, it has had a peculiar position as an art medium.

Part of the prejudice arose because of the old tradition that any printmaking method should necessarily be able to produce large numbers of duplicate prints. This was a handy rule for distinguishing between printmaking and other art forms, such as painting, and because monotypes were single impressions they were often lumped with painting.

Another problem was a certain limitation in the medium itself up to contemporary times; an artist had to work so fast before the ink dried, that often he was denied the length of time necessary to produce a serious work.

One of the better known monotypists of recent times stated the situation in these words — "The monotype had been neglected, considered a print form too uncertain for serious attention. The difficulty lay in the fact that the exposure of the ink dried it in about twenty minutes, time enough for only a feverish spurt of effort. The proof, too, was often spoiled by drying ink."

Since the period of this statement, certain advances have come about which warrant a different attitude toward the "second-rate citizenship" of the monotype.

The problem of time limitation largely has been eliminated, in some cases by the development of slow-drying printing inks, in others by the addition of slow-drying oils where artists' paints are used.

Also, there has been a general change of thinking about what constitutes "quality" in a work of art, more emphasis being placed on creative expressiveness, and less on the drawing of visual detail, which required more time in the doing.

Text continued on page 8   5

Detail of birchbark surface.

Design in Nature. Photographs by Frank Mulvey. Nature, through the action and counteraction of the laws of change, growth, force, and resistance, is a master designer. These photographs are suggestive of the same laws that work for the monotypist, either in the subtle degree found in a precisely ordered print, or one more loosely controlled.

Patterns created by placing drawing ink between two glass slides and pressing them together.

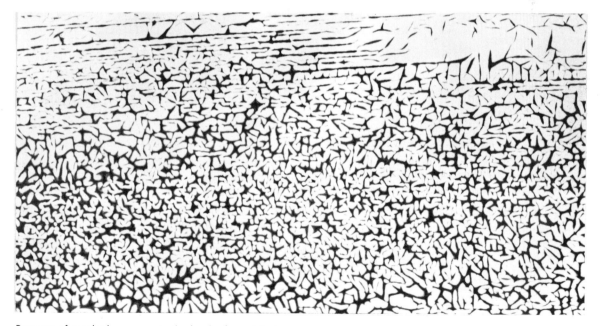

Patterns of cracked mercury on the back of an old mirror.

Another point in favor of the monotype is the leniency that now prevails toward unusual techniques and works in mixed media, and a tolerance for prints and paintings which are not purely one medium or another.

As for the monotype being segregated because it is a "one-print medium," this argument no longer has any meaning. Many etchers and blockprint makers of today also pull only one or two prints from a particular plate. These prints are accepted and even honored for their uniqueness in print showings, so that in fairness, the monotype can no longer be legitimately rejected from exhibitions on the grounds that it is not a method of multiple duplication.

Considering the handicaps connected with the medium, it may seem surprising that there should be such interest and enthusiasm shown for it by its adherents. This can be attributed to the very uniqueness that in some ways is a handicap, but at the same time of beauteous advantage—unusual effects possible of obtainment only by the offset process, and the unfolding of countless facets for individual experimentation.

For textural variety, surface quality, and subtlety of coloration, there is no other medium that can approach the monotype. It is a means of creative invention, surprises, excitement, spontaneity, and organic rightness. Between the original painting on the plate and the finished impression there often takes place a transformation of the crude into the refined, the ordinary into beautiful.

The monotypist learns to draw out and control the laws of cause and effect between the painting and the printing, obtaining results in ways similar to those in which nature would produce them, as seen in a frosted window, sand striations in a desert, erosion-formed canyon cliffs, or in the spectral colorations in a rain-soaked oily street.

The fact that almost no two monotypists use exactly the same methods is illustrative of the immense possibilities for personal expression in the medium. By varying the type of pigments used—oil paints, printers' inks, enamels, and gouache — along with various proportions and kinds of thinners, and the many different kinds of tools, papers, and equipment, innumerable different results can be obtained.

Compared with other printmaking techniques, the preliminary work is simple and direct, can be picked up or left at random, is less costly because of limited space and equipment needed, and the process can be learned quickly without the artist needing to acquire any special knowledge other than that which he already has if he has ever drawn or painted a picture in any of the usual media.

The monotype process can be used for its own sake in purest form, or it can be combined with other techniques and media — painting, drawing, blockprinting, etching, lithography, or photography.

HISTORY OF THE MONOTYPE

The Descent from the Cross. Etching by Rembrandt (the first arched plate), 1633. While it is doubtful that any pure monotypes by Rembrandt exist at the present time, if they ever did, some of the etching proofs show monotype similarities in the manipulation of lights and darks in the inking.

Collection, The British Museum, London.

The story of the discovery and development of the monotype is short, although the small number of its early adherents were nonetheless enthusiastic about its unique potentialities. Perhaps some of this enthusiasm arose because each of the six or seven artists figuring in the little drama believed that he was the true discoverer of the method. As one writer put it, "It has been invented, as a matter of fact, half a dozen times since Castiglione."

To one who has worked to any extent with the medium, the feeling of originality is understandable, for it becomes a personal, creative tool in the hands of each individual using it.

Being a by-product of etching, monotype in the beginning, for the most part, was not considered as a medium to be used for its own sake, but merely as an adjunct to the more orthodox methods of printmaking.

Leonardo did some experiments with transfer methods in his "speculative invention" of accidental blots and stains, and it is claimed by some that certain other Renaissance artists and also Rembrandt knew something of the technique. The author has been unable to substantiate the latter, although some of Rembrandt's etchings show similar effects, which may have been influential in furthering the development of the monotype, as such.

According to all available evidence, however, the honor of first working seriously with the process must go to

Head of an Oriental. Monotype by B. Castiglione.

Flight into Egypt. Monotype by B. Castiglione. Note the lines scratched into the paint in certain areas, delineating the subject and adding richness to the forms.

Collection, Albertina Museum, Vienna.

the Italian historical painter, Giovanni Benedetto Castiglione. Born in Genoa about 1600, Castiglione was a contemporary of Rubens, Van Dyck, and Rembrandt. He studied painting with Giovanni Battista Paggi, Giovanni Andrea de Ferrari, and Van Dyck. Many of his etchings show a distinct resemblance to the style of Rembrandt, and a certain degree of this is carried over into his monotypes, as these were usually of subjects and compositions already carried out in his etchings. He invented the method in Rome, about 1635.

The subjects of Castiglione's monotypes were often illustrative of biblical

The Nativity. Monotype by B. Castiglione.

scenes, as seen in a few of the titles: "The Annunciation to the Shepherds," "Madonna with the Infant Jesus in the Manger," "The Flight into Egypt," and "The Resurrection of Lazarus." Other themes were related to Poussin's pastoral subjects, another of his influences.

According to Augusto Calabi, writing about the monotypes of Castiglione in the *Print Collectors Quarterly* in the twenties, "Castiglione was one of those Italian etchers who liked to employ gray tones and who pulled a limited number of proofs, felt himself irresistibly attracted by complex effects of light and shade in the manner of Rembrandt, and consequently was brought to a deadlock by the incompatibility between his technique and his ideals. Thus the idea occurred to him of concentrating his attention on the second half of his craft —on the inking and printing." His discovery of the monotype came from these experiments in improving his printing technique.

Unidentified Subject. Monotype by B. Castiglione.

Three methods were used by Castiglione. The first one consisted of painting a picture directly on the metal plate and printing it. In the second method, the plate was smeared with ink and the design was scratched out with a pointed stick or similar tool, producing a black background incised with white lines. The third method was a combination of the other two, consisting of painting a picture on the plate and wiping out parts with brush and pointed stick. These three ways are still used by most makers of monotypes up to the present time, along with combining monotype with modern printmaking media such as lithography, blockprinting, and etching.

Consistent with the painting style of his period, the monotypes of Castiglione are lacking in color, in the modern sense, looking much like tinted drawings in some cases, and those done by his second, or scratch method, being practically monochromatic in effect.

After Castiglione's death in 1670 little was done with the monotype until the latter part of the nineteenth century. There is one exception to this in the work of the English artist, William Blake, although here the method often was used not as an end in itself, but as a way of achieving unusual effects in the printing of etchings, or as an underpainting for working over with oils and watercolors.

Blake worked out the process by himself and kept his way of working a secret, enjoying the puzzled conjectures of people who tried to guess how certain effects were obtained. It is said that he printed his relief etchings in a single tint of tawny yellow, green, or blue, and then enriched each impression by hand with glowing color. It is told that he obtained results with which he was fascinated.

Gilchrist's biography relates that a certain person by the name of Tatham explains Blake's methods thus: "When

15

Temporal Eternity. Monotype by B. Castiglione.

Glad Day. Monotype by William Blake.

Collection, British Museum, London.

he wanted to make his prints in oil, he took a piece of millboard and drew his design upon it with some strong, dark ink or color, which he let dry. He then painted on it with oil color in such a fusion that it would blur well, painting roughly and quickly so that the pigment would not have time to dry. After taking a print on paper he finished up the impression with watercolor."

By means of the master outline in ink, Blake was able to wipe off the remains of each printing from the millboard and start over again without redrawing the design, varying the de-

tails of the finished work in the printing and in the watercolor overpainting.

During the 1870's, a new interest in the monotype arose in the United States and in Europe. In Rotterdam in 1879, an American artist, Charles Miller, bought an example, a head of a girl done in soft, impressionistic tones. It was done by I. Ciconi of Milan in 1874. This he showed to fellow members of the Art Club of New York, and later it was exhibited in that city. Soon thereafter a number of artists experimented with the fascinating possibilities of the process.

17

Christ Appearing to the Apostles. Monotype with ink lines added by William Blake.

William M. Chase was the first to exhibit such works in the United States, at the Academy in New York in 1881. In 1882–83 some examples by Peter Moran were included with a show of his etchings held in Philadelphia. Others of the period who experimented with the process included Robert Blum, Frank Duveneck, Henry Sandham, Joseph Lauber, A. H. Bicknell, John S. Sargent, Otto Bacher and the famous actor, Joseph Jefferson.

The process was employed in Duveneck's art classes "as a means of amusement." It was called by them, "Bachertype," after Otto Bacher, whose meth-

ods they used. In 1879–80, in Munich and Florence, Duveneck, Ross Turner, J. W. Alexander, Bacher, and others amused themselves making monotypes at artist club meetings in the evenings. In 1880, James McNeil Whistler and Robert Blum did monotypes in Venice. Whistler employed the method in printing some of his etchings by tinting parts of the surface of his plates, and wiping out lights to obtain certain effects.

One of the reasons for the renewed interest in the process at this period may have been that, although there were many etchers since Rembrandt, few of them up until this time person-

18

Portrait of a Girl. Monotype by Frank Duveneck.

Portrait of a Man. Bachertype (monotype) by Otto Bacher.

Landscape Study. Monotype in sepia tones by Charles A. Walker.

Collection, The Smithsonian Institution, Washington, D. C.

ally carried their work to completion, but instead employed assistants or pupils to do the printing. At the end of the nineteenth century a psychological change took place in which artists began to consider the whole problem of designing, etching, and printing.

About the same time that Chase and others became interested in the monotype process, a Boston artist, Charles A. Walker, discovered it independently. He spent a large part of his time, over eighteen years, in fact, in the making of monotypes, producing several hundred prints.

Walker gave to the process the title "monotype," and although other names have been given to it since, this is the name generally accepted for the method. Walker wrote articles on the subject under the pen name, "Charles A. Coffin."

Another who "invented" the process about this time was James Nasmyth of Turnbridge Wells, originally of Edinburgh. Nasmyth was a manufacturer of machinery and was the inventor of the pile driver and the trip hammer. He devoted his spare time to the monotype, making landscapes and architectural views with the medium.

In 1892 in England, Professor Hubert von Herkomer, an artist and teacher, started experimenting with a method of reproducing large numbers of prints from the metal plate, instead of the usual single duplicate heretofore obtained. He had been introduced to the monotype during a visit to the United States, where an American artist in-

Harvest Time, 1885. Monotype by Charles A. Walker, one of the earliest American monotypists.

Collection, The Smithsonian Institution, Washington, D. C.

trigued him with this form of work, which at that time was a novelty to him.

Herkomer said of the medium: "I know of no method of drawing in pencil or color that can approach the beauty of these printed blacks. The artistic mystery that can be given, the finesse, the depth of tone, and the variety of texture make this manner an almost intoxicating delight to the painter."

Herkomer's special process was called variously "Herkotype," "Herkomergravure," "Spongotype," "Electro-Monotype," and "Plate Printing," and it consisted of making an electrotype plate from the original painting. After long, painstaking trials to find the correct surface for the plates, composition of inks, and the right combination of granulation and conductivity of powder for dusting the plates, Herkomer was

finally successful in perfecting a process by which numerous facsimiles of the original could be produced, the final result being "faithful even in the minutest details."

The plate was sent to the reproducing company while the sticky ink surface was still moist, that is to say within a certain number of days or weeks after execution of the painting. It then was dusted over freely with a fine powder—a compound in which one of the most important ingredients was a metal that was electrically conductible, and which would adhere to every brush mark and every film of ink the artist had placed on the plate. The excess was removed with a large camel's-hair brush, and the painting, coated with as much of the powder as the ink surfaces had taken up, was placed in an electrotyping bath.

22

There, copper was deposited on the surface of the plate, to which the powder had imparted a definite and beautifully varied granulation. After the process of depositing had continued long enough to give to the electrotype a thickness sufficient to prevent its buckling or giving way in the printing process, the plate was removed from the bath and the electrotype stripped off.

What had resulted by this time was a negative of the original plate painting. The powder gave to the paint surface the granulation necessary for effective printing. As the modulations of the original painting were now reversed, a print from this electroplate gave a facsimile of the artist's work.

A similar process was the "galvanograph print" produced by the Germans,

Text continued on page 26

Landscape. Color monotype by Charles A. Walker.

Collection, The Smithsonian Institution, Washington, D. C.

23

Head of an Old Man. Monotype by Sir Hubert Herkomer.

Collection, The Library of Congress, Washington, D. C.

The Album. Monotype in color by Mary Cassatt. Another print of this subject is in the collection of the National Library of France under the title, "Mother and Child."

Collection, Bibliothèque d'Art et d'Archèologie, Paris.

The Foyer. Monotype by Edgar Degas. The original is 16⅔"x23½", and is reputed to be the largest monotype Degas ever made.

Freymann and Schoniger, after a painting by Archterwald, an example of which is in the print collection of the Boston Museum of Fine Arts.

A number of artists in France did some experimenting with the single-impression or true monotype during and after the 1890's, the best known of

these being Lautrec, Corot, Degas, Forain, Pissarro, Renoir, Gauguin, Valadon, and Cassatt. Valadon, and also Adolph Apian, did a form of monotype etching.

Count Lepic, a well-known French painter of the period, made a series of monotypes of landscape subjects. His

26

Cardinal Family. Color monotype by Edgar Degas.

Ballet Master. Monotype by Edgar Degas.

process was to etch outlines of the subject on a metal plate, and then, while the etched lines often completely disappeared in the printing, they were left ready for similar but not exact printings of the same subject.

Of all these artists, Degas most seriously exploited the process, sometimes using it in its pure form, and at other times as underpainting for working over with pastels. It is estimated that he did altogether more than 500 prints.

According to Vollard, in his book *Recollections of a Picture Dealer,* Degas practiced the making of monotypes during moments of after-dinner relaxation. Most of these *plats du jour,* as he called

them, were done at the shop of the printer Cadard, using printers' ink on a copper plate and probably pulled on a printers' proof press.

Gauguin, who also did a considerable number of monotypes, used a method somewhat unusual in that instead of working on a smooth-surfaced plate like most artists, he usually preferred a softer and rather porous one, probably that of a sun-baked clay tile. On top of the softer tones he sometimes added linear accents by tracing through the back of the paper with a pointed stick, at other times working over with pen and ink. They were done in a muted, chromatic scale of ochres, umbers, and browns.

The Nightmare. Monotype by Paul Gauguin.

Heads of Two Tahitian Women. Monotype by Paul Gauguin.

Collection, Cesar de Hauke, Paris.

Natives and Peacock. Monotype by Paul Gauguin.

Collection, The Art Institute of Chicago.

Arearea No Varua Ino. Monotype by Paul Gauguin.

"Modern Spirit and Catholicism" is the title of a little known manuscript by Paul Gauguin which was presented to the City Art Museum of St. Louis a few years ago by the actor, Vincent Price. It consists of writings in black ink on paper, bound in boards decorated with monotypes pasted on the outside and woodcuts on the inside.

Some years later, in the United States, Charles Warren Eaton, Louis Loeb, and Augustus Coopman practiced the art. Loeb, E. Peixotto, and Albert Sterner were among the members of a monotype club formed in New York City, with Leslie Cauldwell as president. Others of this period, around 1908–15, who did work in monotype were Ruel P. Tolman, E. Haskell, C. F. W. Mielatz, Everett Shinn, Maurice Prendergast and Eugene Higgins. Prendergast did many prints in the medium and Higgins continued to do monotypes up to contemporary times.

Eaton showed some monotypes at the exhibition of the American Watercolor Society in 1910, where Everett Shinn also showed several in color which he called "pastel-monotypes."

Mielatz used the process with touches

Text continued on page 34   31

Adoration. Monotype by Paul Gauguin. Front cover of the manuscript, "Modern Spirit and Catholicism."

Virgin and Child. Monotype by Paul Gauguin. Back cover of the manuscript, "Modern Spirit and Catholicism."

Collection, City Art Museum of St. Louis.

Two Heads. Monotype by Paul Gauguin.

Rosenwald Collection, National Gallery of Art, Washington, D. C.

of color in representing certain picturesque spots in New York in a series of plates reproduced in photogravure for the Society of Iconophiles in 1908. He also executed a number of other monotypes, getting interesting effects with a "pigment not intended for art purposes," drawing in broad strokes which contracted when the plate was heated.

Most American painters of the early

1900's were acquainted with the art form, and many of them tried it once or twice out of curiosity, a few of them taking it seriously as a medium of expression.

At that time monotype parties were popular in artists' circles. The painter guests were provided with the proper tools and materials, then a subject was announced and a time limit given. Seated around a large studio worktable,

Text continued on page 42

On the Corso, Rome. Monotype by
Maurice Prendergast.

Courtesy, Kraushaar Galleries, New York.

Orange Market. Monotype by
Maurice Prendergast.

*Collection, Museum of Modern Art,
New York.*

The Rehearsal. Monotype by Maurice Prendergast.

Collection, Museum of Modern Art, New York.

Summer Moon, 1913–14. Monotype by Ruel P. Tolman.

Collection, The Smithsonian Institution, Washington, D. C.

Night, 1913–14. Monotype by Ruel P. Tolman.

Collection, The Smithsonian Institution, Washington, D. C.

The two prints by this artist reproduced here are very small in size, about 3½"x5½", and evidently painted mainly with the thumb and fingers, suggested by the swirls in the sky, and the grooved patterns in the trees and earth.

Summer. Monotype by Charles W. Dahlgreen.

Moonlight Italy. Monotype in black and white by Charles W. Dahlgreen.

Collection, The Smithsonian Institution, Washington, D. C.

The Wandering Jew. Monotype by Eugene Higgins.

The Song of the Shirt. Monotype by Eugene Higgins.

Rogers House, State Street, 1904. Photogravure of a
monotype by Charles Mielatz.

Collection, New York Public Library.

the guests improvised compositions and printed them on an etching press or with a clothes wringer. The results, often extremely interesting, were collected and displayed, and prizes were awarded.

At the Bauhaus, at Weimar, monotype experiments were made by the students in a "materials familiarization course," and also later on at the Institute of Design, in Chicago.

Quite a few artists use monotype for making sketches for painting or sculpture.

Many teachers of various grade levels have added monotype experiments to their programs of art instruction.

The modern trend toward exploitation of media and materials, along with a new freedom from academic ideas of technical purism, brought about a revived interest in the possibilities of indirect techniques such as the monotype. Artists like Matisse, Klee, Picasso, Ernst, Rouault, and de la Fresnaye, in Europe, used such transfer methods, either for monotype prints as such, or for overworking in oil, gouache, or other media.

During the year 1914, Matisse did a series of monotypes in which a black background was incised with thin white lines. They included a variety of subjects—nudes, portraits, still lifes, and

42

Text continued on page 47

Clown With Monkey. Monotype by Georges Rouault.

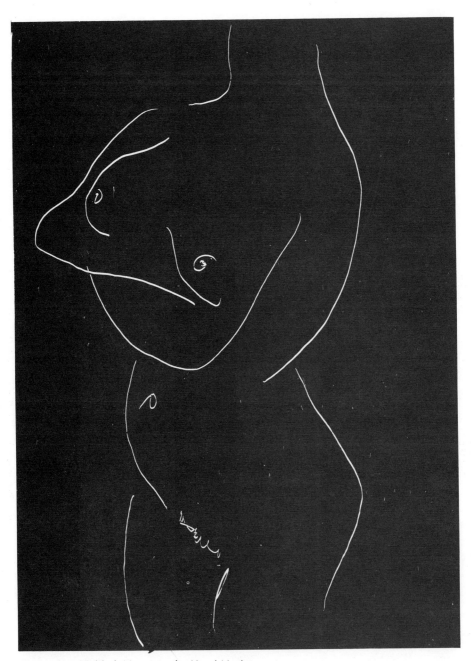

Torso, Arms Folded. Monotype by Henri Matisse.

Collection, Museum of Modern Art, New York.

This kind of print is made by using a brayer and completely covering the plate with black ink, afterward scratching lines into it with a sharp pointed instrument, such as a nail or pointed stick of wood, and making a print from this.

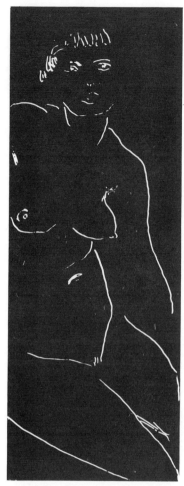

Seated Nude. Monotype by Henri
Matisse.

Private Collection, Philadelphia.

Head of Girl. Monotype by Henri
Matisse. On the back of the
print in Matisse's handwriting it
states that this is his first monotype.

Collection, Louis Macmillan, New York.

Mme André Derain. Monotype by Henri Matisse.

Collection, Robert Thomsen, New York.

45

Street With Carriage. Glass painting by Paul Klee. A picture made on a sheet of glass and framed.

Child Consecrated to Suffering. Oil on canvas by Paul Klee. Textures like those seen here can be made by placing paper on wet paint and pulling it off again.

Room of Contemporary Art, Albright Art Gallery, Buffalo.

interior scenes, and it is said that he was much pleased with these prints.

Paul Klee did a series of "glass paintings" which have all the appearance of monotypes. Actually they are painted on glass in the same way a monotypist would do, but instead of making prints from them, he let them dry on the glass and framed them.

He, of course, obtained some unusual effects in this way, but one wonders at the use of such a fragile material for a painting support.

Klee also used transfer techniques in many of his drawings and paintings.

One of the most consistent of contemporary artists in the use of transfer methods is the French painter, Jean Dubuffet. Many of his oil paintings show this manner of working. He also has invented a technique of pasting monotype-derived cutout shapes together to create striking abstract pictures.

Besides Prendergast and Higgins, already mentioned, several of the early moderns in the United States did monotypes, including "Pop" Hart, John Sloan, Alfred Maurer, and Abraham Walkowitz, the latter using the method to a much greater extent than the others.

Many contemporary Americans have used it, a number of them inventing new procedures to fit their own particular styles of expression. At this time in the history of the subject the combinations of methods and materials becomes so varied that the term "monotype" can no longer be applied to much of the finished work, unless anything done by an indirect, freehand, transfer method

Text continued on page 50   47

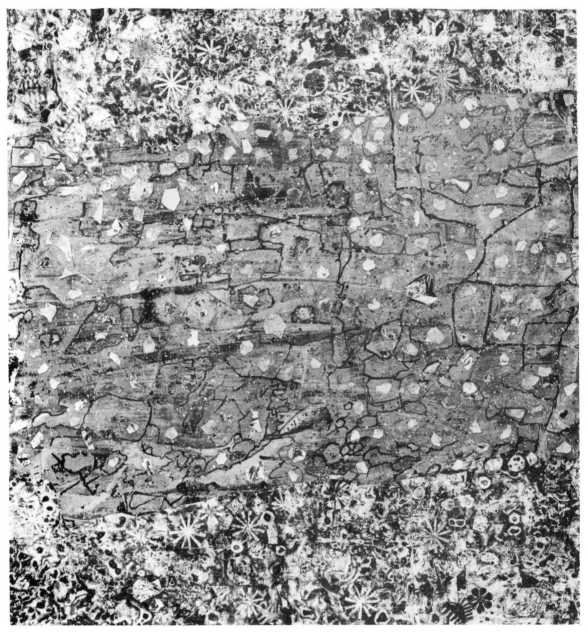

Path Beside the Grass. Oil painting-colláge by Jean Dubuffet. Patterns were cut from paper containing monotype textures, and pasted onto an oil painting on canvas.

Man and Dog. Ink monotype-colláge by Jean Dubuffet.

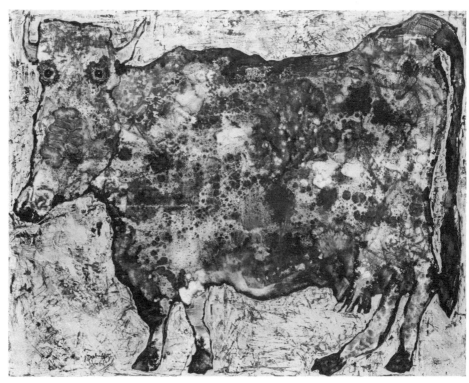

The Cow With the Subtile Nose. Oil and duco on canvas by Jean Dubuffet. A painting showing textures obtained with transfer techniques.

Backyard Band. Monotype by John Sloan.

could loosely be said to come under this heading.

Four examples of original techniques are those of Harry Bertoia, Robert Broner, James Fitzsimmons and Charles Smith, each giving to his particular method a new name.

Bertoia's ways are many, "invention of means according to specific problem" being his creative standard, but his best-known approach is called by him, "prototype," which consists of building up a painting in fairly thick pigment by applying it in gradual steps from cutout shapes made of cardboard, wood, or other materials.

A similar means is that of Charles Smith, whose "block paintings" are a combination of blockprinting and painting. Smith, who learned the craft of woodworking from his father, a patternmaker, keeps on file a large stock of wooden blocks and metal strips in a variety of sizes and shapes, from which he improvises semiabstract compositions.

Robert Broner's "texture imprints" are highly original, being single prints produced from cutouts of variously textured fabrics arranged on a zinc plate and run through an etching press.

An etching plate is first coated with ink of the color decided on for the general background of the design. Then

50

different pieces of fabric are cut in the shape of figures and other subject matter, ink is rolled on them, and they are arranged on the plate. Often there are several different pieces of cloth layered over another.

Next, the printing paper is placed on top, and the whole "sandwich" is rolled through the press. The etching press, through its great pressure, forces the paper down to accept the ink through open mesh fabrics and from the varying surfaces.

Since ink is rolled onto the bare plate and the several superimposed levels of fabrics, the result is a kind of intaglio monotype.

Fitzsimmons' procedures are more complicated, being a mixture of monotype and the lithographic process known

Text continued on page 57

The Poultryman. Color monotype by George O. "Pop" Hart.

Collection, The Smithsonian Institution, Washington, D. C.

51

The Hostess. Color monotype by George O. "Pop" Hart.

Rainy Night. Monotype by John Sloan.

Collection, The Cleveland Museum of Art, Gift of The Print Club of Cleveland.

Mockon Island, Holland, 1906. Monotype in sepia tones by Abraham Walkowitz.

Collection, the Author.

Bathers, 1908. Monotype by Abraham Walkowitz.

Collection, Philadelphia Museum of Art.

54

Harcourt. Monotype by Alfred Maurer.

Deposition. Monotype by Frank J. Van Sloun.

New York Interior. Monotype by Gifford Beal.

Abstraction. Blockpainting by Charles Smith.

as collotype. His earlier work in color photography led him to experiment with liquid dyes and direct printing with gelatin-coated matrixes. Later on his interest changed to using lithographic inks and oil paints, obtaining luminosity by superimposing a number of printed glazes one over the other.

Fitzsimmons calls the finished result a "monoprint," a term which is synonymous with "monotype" in meaning, and except for the fact that the latter is the more popularly accepted term, especially by institutions such as museums and galleries, "monoprint" is perhaps the better of the two. For one reason, there is a typesetting method in the printing trade called "monotype," and this is sometimes confused with the printmaking medium as we know it.

The term, "monoprint," is used by a number of others to describe their individual product, including James Harrison and Buffie Johnson of New York, and Gwyneth King Brown of Princeton, New Jersey. Other titles are "cellocut," so named by Boris Margo of New York, for his kind of process, "monogouache" for the work of Madeline Tourtelot, Chicago, and "multitype" for that of Stella Drabkin, Philadelphia.

The author has developed a technique he calls "monopainting," a distant relative to monotype and very close to

57

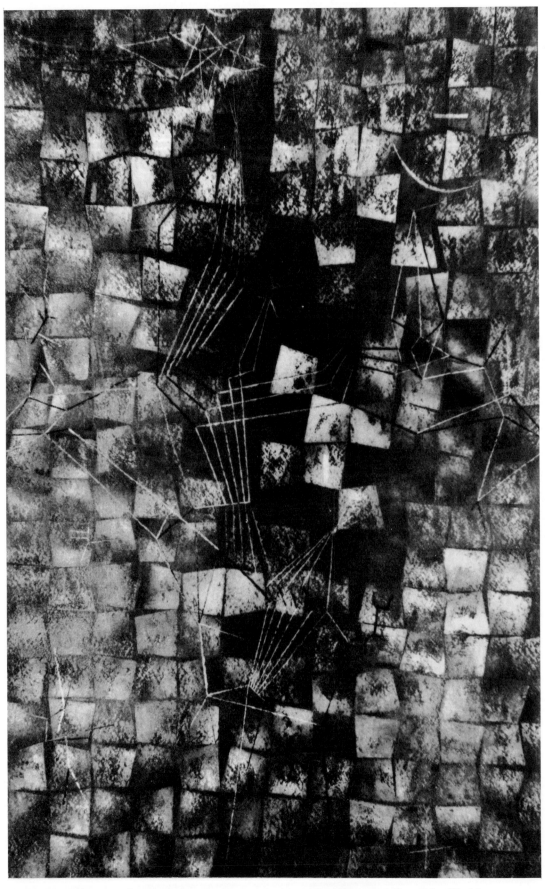

Composition. Prototype by Harry Bertoia. The method used here was to roll a paint-filled brayer across wood or cardboard cutouts, pressing them against the paper, gradually arriving at the final result.

painting. It consists of transferring very thin oils onto slick surfaced papers in a seemingly haphazard, but actually closely controlled use of the accidental. An example of this method can be seen on the end papers of this book. Another West Coast artist, Enid Foster, calls her type of work "monopen," it being a combination of monotype and pen drawing.

One of the oddest forms of print-making the author has run across is the "floatagraph," practiced by Henry N. Bagley and Wilson Irvine, several examples of which are in the collection of the Smithsonian Institution in Washington.

It consists of floating paint on water and transferring it to paper in a controlled manner.

Many modernists in the field of etching use procedures similar to monotype for obtaining different textural and other effects. The well-known etchers William Stanley Hayter and Mauricio Lasansky have done outstanding work in this direction, as well as in teaching their methods to others.

A new color etching process evolving out of monotype techniques is that of Milton Goldstein, of Flushing, New York. His method consists of making a monotype with oil crayons and printing

Interacting Forms II. Monoprint by James Fitzsimmons.

Collection, Société Anonyme, Yale University Art Gallery.

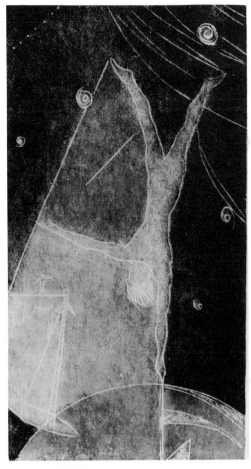

Acrobat. Multitype by Stella Drabkin. Five overlay printings were used to achieve the final result. Printed on white Goyu paper with an etching press.

over this with one or more impressions of printing inks mixed with a transparent base such as that used in serigraphy.

Another unique method is one used by educator Berne Biteman of Seattle, Washington, who has been successful in teaching it to his elementary pupils. Airplane glue is used to make line drawings on a glass surface, after which the glue is allowed to dry until it is hard. A piece of paper is then placed over the design and an inked roller run over the back of the paper, picking up an impression of the line drawing.

This is similar to the "frottages" of Max Ernst, who made lead pencil rubbings of leaves, linen, brush strokes of a painting, thread on a spool, and other natural textures. He used it, of course, as a technical means toward an imaginative, surrealistic end, discovering readymade surfaces, rather than creating a line design beforehand, as in Biteman's method.

An expert in the craft of making rubbings is Hsuan Chang, former professor of archaeology and philology, New Asia College, Hong Kong. He represents the third generation in a family

Fruit Life. Multitype by Stella Drabkin. A monotype produced with six overlays. Printed on yellow Mulberry paper with a mixture of oil paint and retouch varnish, using a Plexiglas plate and run through an etching press.

Landscape. Floatagraph by Henry N. Bagley.

A highly unusual form of printmaking, almost identical with that used in making marbled paper for bookbindings. A tub is filled with water, onto the surface of which liquid oil paints in various colors are dropped. These are then stirred around and intermingled in a controlled manner until a desirable pattern is obtained, after which a sheet of paper is laid upon the surface. Upon removal of this sheet, which takes the colors with it, the picture is printed. By blocking out certain areas on the paper with rubber cement, and by overlay printing, one is able to control the patterns and tones according to the pictorial need.

Hills and Sky. Floatagraph by Wilson Irvine.

of professionals doing this kind of work, specializing in reproducing sculptural bas-reliefs, tomb inscriptions, incised designs, and other works of art.

A few artists have used monotypes in magazine and book illustration. Paul Bransom, the animal illustrator, is known for his story illustrations in this medium. Virginia Kaar has used it almost exclusively for illustrating genre subjects and children's stories. Cyrus Leroy Baldridge and Alexander Dobkin also have done illustrations in monotype.

Besides the European artists men-

tioned earlier, the names of several other foreign workers in monotype have become known in this country, such as Margaret Preston of Australia, Bella Leme, Lino Eneas Spilimbergo, and Candido Portinari of Brazil, and Demetrio Urruchua of Argentina.

A list of contemporary Americans having seriously explored the medium, producing large numbers of prints, would include such names as Harry Bertoia, Boris Margo, Adja Yunkers, Buffie Johnson, Fritz Eichenberg, Hedda Sterne, Israel Abramofsky, Gwyneth King Brown, Salvatore S. Meo, Theresa

Text continued on page 66   63

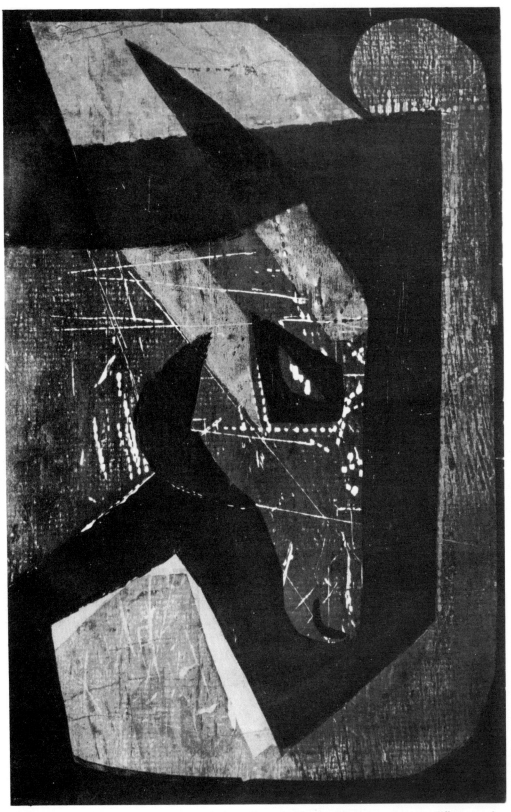

Animal Profile. Monoprint from woodblocks by Milton Goldstein. Made by using six different color overlays.

Donna McIntyre makes a large crayon sketch.

The lines begin to appear under the brayer.

After placing sketch underneath the plate, Mike Baker, following the lines, applies airplane cement to the glass.

Students co-operate in hanging monotype exhibit.

Under the supervision of Berne Biteman, sixth graders of the Seward School, Seattle, make monotypes as a class project. After making a design on the glass plate with airplane cement, it is allowed to dry, then paper is placed over it and an ink covered brayer is run across the back, picking up the design.

Hsuan Chang making a rubbing.

Photograph of a rubbing in three dimensions by Hsuan Chang. The original object from which the rubbing was made is a *Ting,* an ancient Chinese bronze tripod. At the top is seen a rubbing of the inscription from the inside of the *Ting.*

Bernstein, Henry Nordhausen, and Abraham Hankins, all of them residing in the Eastern states. In the Midwest there are Madeline Tourtelot, Robert Broner, Don Baum, Dwight Kirsch, and Robert K. Sterner. In the West are Frank Van Sloun, Albert Patecky, Howard B. Schleeter, and Enid Foster.

The late Seth Hoffman made a career of working with the monotype, devoting years to perfecting his control of the ink, and the delicate manipulation required in the proofing.

In Hoffman's case, his having worked as a sculptor was an asset, for his three-

dimensional forms were modeled mainly with the thumb, directly out of a layer of printers' ink spread on the glass plate.

His work exemplifies the extreme in strict control of the subtractive method, leaving little to chance in the end result.

After a good deal of experimenting, he narrowed his materials down to a very permanent cream-colored Japanese etching paper, very soft, heavily textured, with a rough and smooth side. This paper he found to be sensitive, highly absorbent, and especially receptive to monotype inking.

Hoffman also had a special ink made

66

Text continued on page 87

White Doom. Monotype by Paul Bransom. This artist has used monotypes for illustrating stories in several nationally known magazines.

A Group of Monotypes by Contemporary Australians

Billabong. Monotype by Margaret Preston.

Scrub Country. Monotype by Margaret Preston.

Dead Sea Bird. Monotype by Clifton Pugh.

Forms in Landscape. Monotype by Henry Salkauskas.

Phoenix. Gouache monotype by Allen David.

Composition. Monotype by Leslie Lawson.

Head of an Indian. Monotype by Lino Eneas Spilembergo.

Collection, Museum of Modern Art, New York.

72

The Serpent. Monotype by Demetrio Urruchua.

Collection, Museum of Modern Art, New York.

The Beast. Monotype by Demetrio Urruchua.

Collection, Museum of Modern Art, New York.

Dancer. Monotype by Bella Leme.

Collection, New York Public Library.

Portrait of Adalgisa Nary. Monotype in sepia by Candido Portinari.

Collection, Museum of Modern Art, New York.

Still Life. Monotype by Leonica Rivacova.

Queen of Sheba. Monotype by Etienne Ret.

Collection, Mr. and Mrs. Leslie Flowers, San Antonio.

Mediterranean. Monotype by Jean Boudal.

77

Three Personages, 1951. Monotype by Adja Yunkers. Printed on wrapping paper that had been coated with an all-over film of deep blue color applied with a brayer, and while still wet, the lines were drawn with a turpentine-filled brush. After each stroke, a blotter was used to pick up the excess thinner and give the offset textures similar to those found in more traditional monotypes.

The Visitation. Monotype by Fritz Eichenberg.

Charity. Monotype by Fritz Eichenberg.

Old Man. Monotype on Fiberglas by Israel Abramofsky. Painted with oil paints on oilcloth and transferred to a sheet of thinly woven fiberglass. Much of the unusual quality of these monotypes by Abramofsky is lost in reproduction.

Still Life. Monotype on colored suede paper by Israel Abramofsky. Painted on canvas board and printed on undampened suede paper, using the back of a hairbrush and a spoon for rubbing.

Machine (4), 1949. Monotype by Hedda Sterne. Technically, this could be called a transfer drawing, as it was made by coating the plate with paint, then after placing paper over it, the design was drawn on the back of the paper, the paint adhering to the underside wherever pressure was applied.

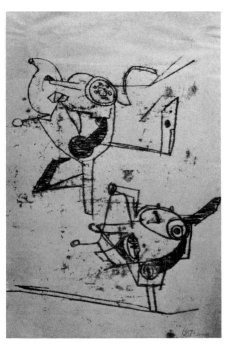

Produced in the same way as Machine (4) by the same artist, except that there, besides the line drawing, tonal areas were added by rubbing the back of the paper with the fingers.

Machine, 1949. Monotype by Hedda Sterne.

82

Noumenon. Monoprint by Buffie Johnson. Here, thick, light keyed oil paint was transferred onto dark paper, helping to create a mood of quiet mystery.

Monoprint by Buffie Johnson.

Imago. Monoprint by Buffie Johnson.

New York Street. Color monotype by Theresa Bernstein.

In the Dressing Room. Monotype by Seth Hoffman.

The Challenger, 1929. Monotype by Seth Hoffman.

up for him by the Sleight Metalic Ink Company of Philadelphia. Its number was 4795-48326, Process Black, and was put up in tubes.

Other Americans who have done fewer, but nonetheless serious experiments are Will Barnet, Ernest Newman, Richard Lahey, Ann Ryan, Xavier Barile, Moses Soyer, Antonio Frasconi, Karl Schrag, Louis Schanker, Worden Day, Seong Moy, Minna Citron, and Pennerton West of the East Coast; Adrian Troy, Robert McLaren, and Paul Ashby of the Midwest; Jacob Elshin, Louis Bunce, and Ambrose Patterson of the Northwest, and Robert Miller and John Kjargaard of Hawaii.

In 1940, Ashby organized the American Monotype Society, under whose sponsorship a group of monotypists showed their work in traveling exhibitions. The group has since disbanded.

In this country, as well as abroad, other artists, too numerous to mention by name, have produced monotypes. Many others have used similar transfer techniques to produce unusual effects in several kinds of printmaking, and in the painting of easel pictures and larger works such as murals.

Text continued on page 95

Rising Sun. Color monotype by Richard Lahey.

Praying Figure. Color monotype by
William Gropper.

*Collection, Whitney Museum of American Art,
New York.*

Roan Stallion. Monotype by Max Kahn.

Night Woods. Monotype by Pennerton West.

Haiten Plains No. 1. Monotype by Pennerton West.

The Sculptor (Chaim Gross). Monotype by Moses Soyer.

Dancer Seated. Monotype in browns by Moses Soyer.

In The Studio. Monotype retouched with pastel by Moses Soyer.

Dancers. Monotype by Ambrose Patterson. Here is seen a slightly different approach, in the white silhouette of the figures against a dark background.

MATERIALS AND EQUIPMENT

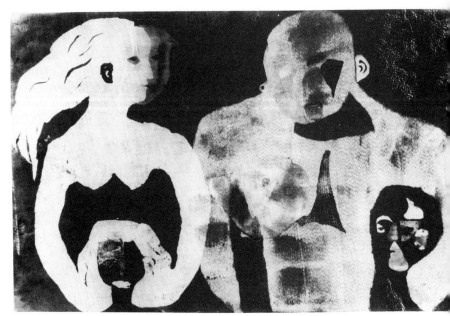

Artist With Family. Texture Imprint by Robert Broner. Shapes of figures printed from cutouts of a variety of woven fabrics.

Collection, New York Public Library.

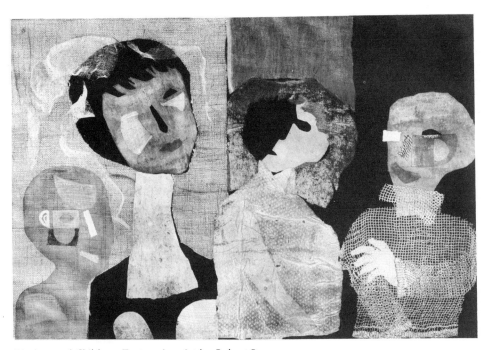

Mother and Children. Texture Imprint by Robert Broner.

Collection, Mr. and Mrs. Hugh Reynolds, San Francisco.

94

Before going into the details of several typical methods of producing transfer prints and paintings, the reader can get a clearer understanding of this after first becoming acquainted with some of the materials and equipment aspects of the problem.

PLATES

The plate is the surface on which the design is originally painted and is usually of a hard, smooth nature. The first monotypes were done on etching plates of copper or zinc. These are still popular with many artists because they can be put under heavy pressure while printing and are likewise not breakable in handling.

Of the two, zinc is usually preferred, because of the lighter, more neutral. tone, as a background for painting the picture. The backs of old etching plates can be used for making monotypes.

Some artists prefer the smoother surface of glass to that of metal for use as a plate. One advantage of glass is that a sketch can be placed underneath the transparent plate and copied or followed with ease, or the design can be sketched on one side of the glass in lithographic crayon, then turned over and the painting carried out by following the outlines of the sketch. Heavy plate glass is better to use than the thinner variety because of its greater strength and durability.

The transparency of glass is an asset in another way, because it can be placed over some sort of light-toned paper while the picture is being painted, thus simulating the appearance of canvas, on which an artist is used to working. A piece of heavy milk glass having an opaque white or cream tone eliminates the necessity of using the light-toned paper as a background, but has the disadvantages of other nontransparent plates.

Celluloid and plastic are surfaces with the advantage of transparency, while also having the durability of metal under pressure. These materials might well replace glass as a plate material. Their only drawback is their softer surface, which may pick up scratches and other marks over a period of time, although some artists prefer a bit of tooth on the plate, rather than too much slickness.

Plates can be made of wood or linoleum blocks, which are especially adaptable to making a number of similar but varied prints from the same design, by drawing it on the block in water-soluble ink, and after this dries, painting the plate in the usual way and printing it, the excess paint being wiped off after each print, but leaving the design for subsequent painting and printing. End-grain maple makes a fine plate for transfer drawings.

Hard-surface plates, such as metal, wood, fiberboard, or glass, are necessary for printing on paper and other pliable materials because, in order for the pigment to transfer from one surface to another, one of the surfaces must have a certain amount of give.

In other words, in handwork, where great pressures are not used and where subtle textural effects are desired, one of the two surfaces that come together to make the impression should be more pliable than the other. In the case of the hard plate, it presses onto the paper, the paper gives with the pressure and the surface nap picks up the pigment and holds it.

The reverse of this can be done by using a pliable plate from which a design can be transferred to a hard surface. Oilcloth makes an excellent pliable plate, to be used for obtaining offset effects on paintings where wood, canvas, fiberboard, or other hard-backed material is to receive the impression. Murals and other large areas may be painted in this way.

MEDIA

By "media" is meant the several combinations of pigment and binder, or vehicle, which the artist uses to paint the design on the plate, such as oil paints, watercolors, and the like.

Most of the usual media of artists and printmakers can be used for making monotypes. Printing inks and artists' oil paints are the most popular of these. Others are etching inks, transparent watercolors, gouache, tempera, dyes, and wax crayons.

Printers' and lithographers' inks can be obtained from commercial dealers in a variety of colors. They differ from artists' paints in that they contain a certain amount of varnish and drier, which makes them more transparent and stiffer in consistency. The pigments used in these inks are more finely ground than those in artists' oil paints, also adding to the transparency.

Because of these qualities, printers'

96

inks can be smeared or rolled out very thinly on the plate for scratching out lines and tones where the artist's interest is in careful drawing. The stiffness of printers' inks requires fairly heavy pressures in printing, so that if a mechanical press is not used, quite a little effort is needed, using a steel hand roller, the back of the bowl of a spoon, or other hard instrument.

Etchers' and blockprinters' inks are very good for most purposes, but they also need heavy pressures in printing.

Oil paints need less pressure in making the impression, and are perhaps the most often used of any vehicle. They are highly versatile, for they can be used in the thick consistency as they come from the tube or thinned by several means, for achieving a variety of effects.

In this chapter a number of secondary quality materials are listed for the benefit of teachers with classroom projects, and others who wish to use less expensive materials for trial experiments. Wherever these are mentioned their inferiority is noted. For professional work, of course, the artist will want to use only high-quality materials for ultimate permanency.

Ordinary house paints can be used, but they are inferior to artists' paints in quality, usually contain a cheap grade of oil that yellows and darkens with age, and for serious work should be replaced by artists' colors.

Silk-screen paints are usually somewhat better in quality than house paints, but so little is used for printing on small areas, such as standard-size papers, that it does not seem worth while for either the professional or amateur to use anything less than the best artists' paints, where oil is the medium. The smooth, mat quality of silk-screen paints can be duplicated by adding some silk-screen extender to oil paints.

A good grade of synthetic enamel such as that used for painting automobile bodies can be used in transfer processes for easel paintings or on larger areas such as fiberboard panels or wall murals. These are fairly permanent, depending on the particular colors used.

Opaque watercolors such as gouache or poster colors give excellent results on absorbent papers which have been prepared by dampening before using. Transparent watercolors are usable, but work better when something like starch is added to give them body and traction.

Interesting results can be obtained with lithographic and wax crayons, although these require special processes in making the impression, which will be considered later.

THINNERS · BINDERS DRIERS

A thinner is a liquid solvent used to dilute or thin a pigment such as oil or ink. The usual thinners for oil paints are turpentine, kerosene, or some good quality commercial paint thinner. That for watercolors, casein, or gouache, of course, is water.

Of the oil paint and printing ink thinners, kerosene is for most purposes better than turpentine, because it has less odor, is slower in drying on the plate, more oily and smoother in substance, and easier on the hands. Otherwise, where one is making the impression on nonabsorbent material such as fiberboard or canvas, the faster-drying qualities of turpentine are preferable, if any thinner at all is used.

Some of the commercial printing ink thinners have the precise ingredients necessary for thinning particular kinds of inks, and the monotypist may decide after a little experimenting whether or not these are better than kerosene or turpentine for his uses.

A binder is a liquid substance mixed with colored pigments to give them fluidity in the painting of a design or picture and which, after being applied, dries and holds the particles of pigment together on the surface of the canvas, paper or other material.

The number of binders for water-soluble paints is limited, the main ones being gum arabic, glue, and starches made from wheat, corn, or rice. Starch tends to give body and adhesiveness to watercolor and gouache paints for offset work. A drop or two of glycerin may be added to water-soluble paints to give them greater flowing action.

For oil painting in general, linseed oil is the standard binder, so that most of the oil paints that the monotypist uses are likely to contain this as the binder. If any more binder is added to oil paints other than that already in them as they come out of the tube, for printing on paper, slower drying oils may be preferred. These oils are more colorless, and they stay in soluble condition over a period of many hours while the picture is being worked on, then after the impression is made they dry quite readily because of the absorbent qualities of the paper. For work on less absorbent surfaces, linseed oil would dry more quickly.

A list of slow-drying oils would include mineral oil, poppy oil, vegetable oil (salad oil), baby oil, and machine oil. Refined poppy oil is the only permanent one among this group.

An extender is a medium which, when added to paint, extends or expands the volume, but at the same time does not necessarily thin its consistency.

Certain commercial products, such as textile and silk-screen paint extenders, can be added to oil paints, lending more tractability and body to them. These usually contain some kind of bodying agent such as Bentone, varnish, and drier. For serious work one should be careful and knowledgeable about the contents of commercial paints.

A drier is a special liquid sometimes mixed with paints to make them dry faster. Most enamels contain a certain amount of it.

Refined boiled linseed oil, stand oil,

sun-thickened oil, retouching varnish, artists' Copal or Dammar varnish, and Japan drier are some of the media which may be added to oil paints or printing inks, particularly where transparent overlay printing is done, or where hard-surface panels or other materials are used for receiving the impression.

TOOLS

Hog's hair and sable brushes are the primary tools of the monotypist, as with the easel painter. They are used to paint the design on the plate in about the same way as painting a picture on canvas, except that the monotypist becomes more aware of the patterning of the brush strokes as the pigment is applied or scraped off, for all the details of this will be emphasized in the impression.

Various kinds of fabrics are helpful in obtaining textural richness. Wads of cotton or other soft cloth can be used for blending or wiping out certain areas. Any lint-free material such as silk, rayon, muslin, marquisette, etc., is good for texturing or wiping out.

For drawing lines or picking out highlights or other fine details of a picture, sharpened sticks made of soft wood, such as matches or toothpicks, work very well. Hard woods or metals sometimes scratch into the surface of the plate, especially if it happens to be of zinc, copper, plastic, or wood.

There is no limit to the kinds of tools which can be used to create different forms and effects—sponges, combs, tongue depressors, pieces of cardboard, children's blocks, toothbrushes, chains, and many more.

The thumb and fingers make fine tools, some artists using these almost exclusively. Others use cloth wrapped around the index finger for particular effects.

PRESSES

The standard way of making a monotype impression by mechanical means is with the etching press, and it is used more or less in the same way as in making an etching. Where an etching press is not available, a letter or blockprint press will serve the purpose, depending on the stiffness of the paint being used. With a little practice a hand-powered clothes-wringer will do an excellent job of printing.

For printing from a plate containing a stiff printers' or etchers' ink, some sort of mechanical press is a time and energy saver, although not indispensable; in fact it is not the preference of many artists. A steel roller will bring out a good impression, as will rubbing the back of a tablespoon over the reverse side of the printing paper after it is laid on the inked plate.

If the design is painted in more soluble pigments, less pressure is necessary. In this case one can use a rubber roller

How to Make a Barin

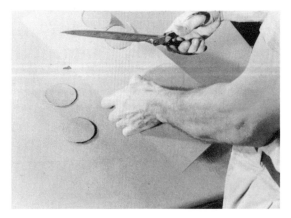

1. Cut several disks from heavy cardboard.

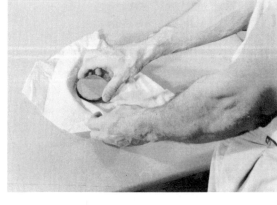

4. Place disks in piece of cloth with rounded edge down.

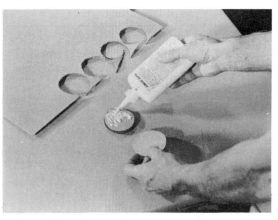

2. Glue the disks together.

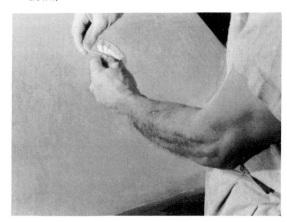

5. Draw cloth up tightly and wrap with string.

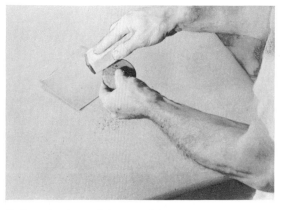

3. Round edges of bottom disks with sandpaper.

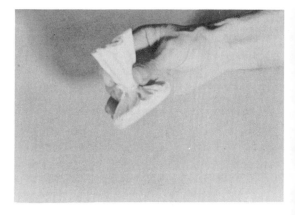

6. Leaving a couple of inches of cloth for a handle, trim the excess and the barin is ready for use.

or blockprint brayer, a soft cloth, or merely the fingers or palm of the hand.

A barin, a special pad which can be made by covering a few cardboard disks with cloth, is useful when a press is not available, and is especially good for printing crayon or watercolor-pencil monotypes.

PAPERS

There are many different kinds of papers on which good results can be obtained in printing a monotype. The kind of paper to be used depends on the particular combination of the several factors involved: the medium—oils, printing inks, or watercolors; the consistency of the pigment—thick, thin, stiff, or other; the method of printing —with a mechanical press or by hand; and the particular result desired—style of form, textural effect, and so on. With all these things in mind, the final selection of the right paper can be determined after a certain amount of individual experimentation.

The Japanese, Indian, or Chinese rice papers are perhaps the choice all-around ones to print on, regardless of the medium, style, or printing method used. Other soft-surface papers from which one might make a selection are charcoal, watercolor, and blotter.

The various high-quality papers used by etchers, blockprinters, lithographers, and engravers give the monotypist a wide selection.

There are some good-quality tissue papers that give interesting results. These usually can be purchased in various tones and colors from some company specializing in Oriental papers. Some beautiful effects can be obtained on black or very dark papers of this sort, using white paint or printing ink. Other thin papers like onionskin, florists' tissue, and tracing paper can be used to advantage for less serious work.

Slick-surface papers such as Cameo, shelf paper, fingerpainting paper, and tracing paper are excellent for particular effects. The former is the most permanent of the four.

In the category of hard-surface papers there are, among numerous others, two- or three-ply Strathmore kid, Howells handmade papers, pencil drawing paper, eighty-pound coated-stock printers' paper, illustration board, and a lithographers' paper named Basinwerks.

Some of the cover papers used for binding pamphlets and house organs are very good for printmaking. Unusual textures sometimes can be found in this category, as well as a large choice of colors and whites. These papers are available at the wholesale houses of the larger manufacturers. If one finds it difficult to persuade such sources to sell small amounts, it may be secured through some friendly printer or some other wholesale buyer.

To be of practical value, any paper used should be strong enough to withstand dampening and printing without tearing or disintegrating in the process, if one prints on dampened paper, which is the rule in making monotypes.

There are many different kinds and grades of Oriental papers to choose from—Linweave Japan, Shoji (a hand-made paper with a slight tint), Moriki, Mulberry, Osaka (a velvety paper), Okawara, Natsuma White, Goyu, Zebu White and so on.

Two of the largest U. S. importers of Oriental papers are the Stevens-Nelson Company, 7-11 Laight Street, New York City, and Yashutomo and Company, 24 California Street, San Francisco.

So much depends on the particular use to which a paper will be put that the best advice one can give is for the artist to experiment with a variety of papers, to find the ones that fit his individual needs.

SUMMARY OF BASIC MATERIALS

The beginner should assemble at least the following materials and equipment before starting to make monotypes:

Plate   A piece of metal, fiber-board, plastic, or glass, two or three inches larger all around than the size of the paper to be used for printing.

Media   Oil paint or printers' ink in black, umber, or colors.

Thinner   Turpentine or kerosene, for thinning the ink and cleaning the brushes and equipment.

Tools   Artists' bristle brushes in three or four different sizes, from one inch down to one-eighth inch in width. Two or three pointed sable brushes in various sizes. A flat house-painters' brush about one inch in width.

Presses   Two small, hard block-print brayers, one for rolling out ink on the plate or palette, one for pressing the back of the printing paper to transfer the design. A spoon for certain kinds of transfer.

Palette   A flat piece of glass, tin, or other nonabsorbent material for use in mixing colors or rolling out ink before applying.

Cotton   Several wads of cotton batting and small pieces of cloth for wiping out ink when painting the design on the plate.

Sticks   Several wooden sticks, matches, or toothpicks for drawing lines in the paint or ink on the plate.

Paint Rags   Enough for keeping the hands and equipment clean.

Newspapers   Place these underneath the printing plate as a buffer against the table or drawing desk, and to help hold the plate from sliding.

Printing Paper   Several sheets of soft paper on which to print the monotypes.

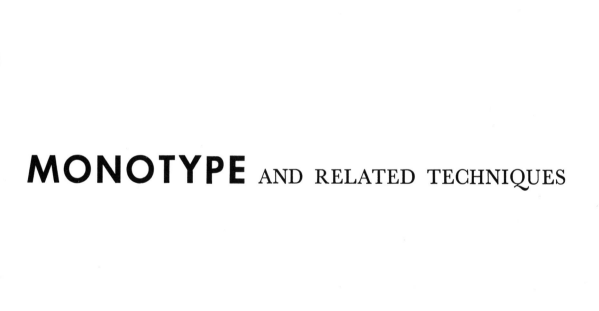

MONOTYPE AND RELATED TECHNIQUES

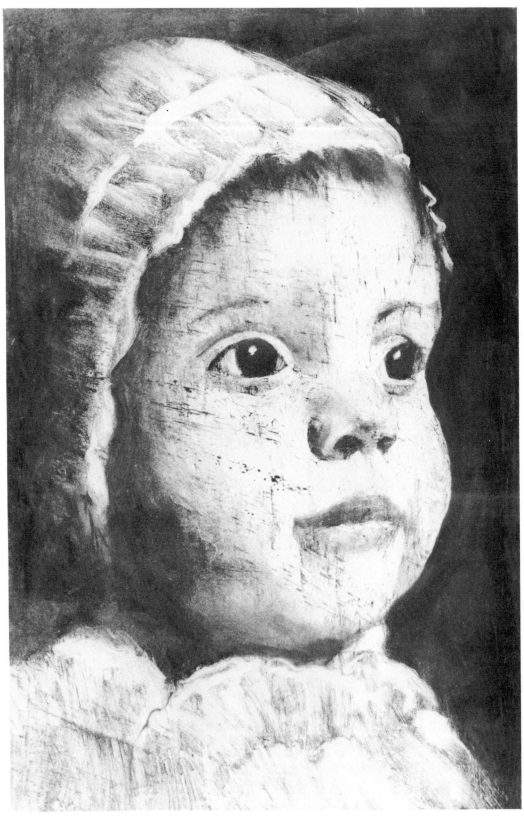

Angelina. Monotype by Seth Hoffman. An example of the subtractive tonal method.

It is recommended that this chapter be read completely through before choosing any particular approach for experimentation, especially if the reader is a novice.

As mentioned in an earlier chapter, there are three principal methods of making a monotype. These may be termed the additive, the subtractive, and a combination of the two. In the additive method the original design is painted by adding or building up pigment, usually in full color, onto the surface of the plate, and then transferring this to paper or other material.

The subtractive method is to smear the whole surface of the plate with paint or ink, and to scratch or wipe out the design with rags, brushes, sticks, or other tools. The subtractive method is more nearly related to drawing, while the additive is closer to that of painting. The control in each process can be heightened or lessened to suit the particular need by varying the consistency of the pigment and the type of paper used.

Considering the many different kinds of materials and equipment from which an artist may make a selection, along with the choice of one or a combination of methods of making a monotype, plus his individual preferences in taste and style of approach, there are almost no limits to the creative possibilities for the artist in the monotype medium. This is one of its attractive features— the opportunity for free invention and experimentation toward the individual's expression of form and mood.

SUBTRACTIVE METHOD

The subtractive is the original and traditional way of making monotypes,

A six year old child makes a lineal monotype, suggesting the ease in using this
method.

1. A coat of dark ink or paint is rolled onto the
plate.

2. Using a wooden stick, the lines are scratched into
the paint.

3. A piece of absorbent paper is laid upon the
picture.

and perhaps the first one that the novice should try.

If less space is given to it here, it is not that it is less important, but because of its rather set and definite aim toward perfect control, it rules out various experimental side roads that other, looser methods do not.

This method is one in which drawing and modeling are of foremost importance, and it lends itself especially to the kind of form that is essentially three dimensional.

The artist to whom fine drawing is appealing usually prefers a skillful control over the medium, instead of relying on the happy accidental effects obtainable in certain other methods. Of course one can vary the degree of surety in either, but generally speaking, the subtractive method is best adapted to precise draftsmanship and sure control.

The type of pigment used is an important factor in reducing or expanding the possibility of accidental effects, oil paints tending to spread and blot, while stiff printers' inks do not.

As pointed out before, the subtractive technique lends itself especially to making monochromatic, rather than full-color prints, although some skillful artists do use it in full color. The pigment ordinarily used for monochromatic monotypes is black, of course, but the kind of black can be varied from a cold bluish one to one of great warmth and richness, by adding a touch of blue or green to the mixture for the cooler blacks, or for the warmer ones adding burnt or raw sienna, burnt or raw umber, or some other type of warm color. If oil paints are used for the subtractive method, the mixture can be stiffened with the addition of a little stand oil or varnish.

With the subtractive method, the sketch from which the design is copied cannot be followed very well by placing it under the plate, as the whole of this is smeared over with ink, and the sketch would not be visible. Instead, a plain piece of white paper is laid underneath, so that the lines and tones will be clearly seen as they are scratched or wiped out. A few sheets of blotter or newsprint underneath the white paper make a buffer for the plate to rest on.

Milk-white glass is probably the best type of plate to use for this kind of monotype, and can be purchased at most glass dealers. It is necessary for this to be of heavy plate glass, if a mechanical press is to be used. Even then, great care must be taken not to break it with too much pressure.

SUBTRACTIVE LINEAL MONOTYPES

A very simple way to use the subtractive method, and one that would be an easy introduction to working in monotype, is that illustrated in the line drawings by Henri Matisse, pages 44-45. Here, lines are scratched in the all over coat of black ink on the plate, the end result being pure black and white, without shading of any kind.

4. The picture is transferred to the paper by rubbing the back with a spoon.

5. The print is pulled from the plate.

6. Lauren Tye proudly surveys the result.

Making a black and white lineal monotype is so easy that little explanation is necessary, except that given in the step-by-step demonstration photographs on this subject. However, it is better first to read the procedure for making a print where halftones are used, before attempting it.

Beginners should work fairly small, say 8" x 10" or 9" x 12", as larger prints are hard to handle.

It is assumed that the artist has prepared a sketch to work from, or at least has an idea in mind before starting.

The finished print will be reversed from the way that the sketch is drawn, and this should be taken into account when the design is made. Check the way it will look in reverse by holding the sketch up to a mirror at intervals during its development or after it is finished.

After setting out the oil paints on the palette and readying the paintbrushes, rags, and other equipment, but before proceeding with the painting, prepare the paper for the printing. If the paper being used is one with a slick surface, there will be no need for any preparation except to have it near at hand. If it does not have a slick surface, it usually should be soaked in water for a time before using, although some few artists prefer it dry.

The length of soaking time depends on the absorbency of the particular kind of paper being used; the soft, Oriental ones or blotting paper for

instance, would need very little. Some hard-surface papers, on the other hand, need to be soaked several hours or overnight before use. The correct timing is important, but that will improve with experience.

Before putting the paper to soak in tray, sink, or bathtub, mark the rough and smooth sides, for after dampening, it is difficult to tell which is the correct side for printing.

If the paper has a watermark, it will be readable from the correct side. If it does not have a watermark, look for the side on which the surface is slightly rougher and less mechanical in texture.

Some artists purposely may choose to print on the back of the paper, which is perfectly all right. In any case, it is still a good idea to mark the side to be used before soaking it. The paper also should be cut to the right size before wetting, allowing a fair-size margin for matting.

SUBTRACTIVE TONAL MONOTYPES

To proceed with the making of a tonal monotype by the subtractive method, squeeze out a small daub of ink onto the plate and spread it out with a brayer, brush, cloth pad, or the fingers until it makes an allover, uniform layer. This will serve as a middle tone, so it should not be either too heavy or too light, somewhat thinner than for ordinary printing of etchings. Make the drawing by wiping out the lighter tones with a cloth or cotton

108

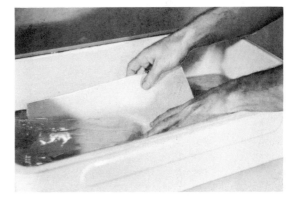

Steps in dampening paper for printing.

3. The pieces are placed in a receptacle of water, being sure that no dry pockets remain between sheets.

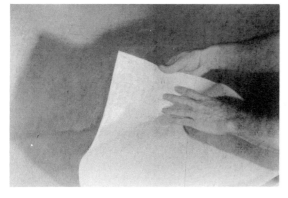

1. The paper is examined to determine the correct side.

4. After a thorough soaking, the length of time depending on the kind of paper being used, it is then lifted out a sheet at a time and the excess water drained off.

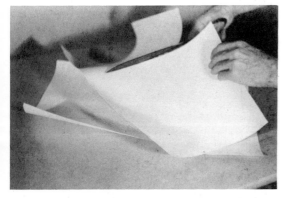

2. It is cut into sizes slightly larger than the design to be printed.

5. Individual pieces are stacked between sheets of newsprint or blotting paper, after which they are ready for use.

1. Artist's bristle
brush.

2. Wooden sticks.

3. Fingers.

4. Paint spatula.

Effects produced with various tools in making a tonal monotype.

Cloth.

6. Cotton wad.

pad, bristle brush, fingernail, fingers, or sharpened stick, and by adding more ink for the darks. It usually works better to do the dark areas last, the same as with the additive method.

Each kind of material used for the cloth pad will create a particular quality of texture, as will the other tools—palette knife, flat or pointed sticks, cotton swabs, flat bristle brushes, and so on.

In this method the finger will give linear, engraved-line effects; the cotton dabber affords soft, smooth textures; the bristle brush produces stippled, broken tones. Crisp, sharp highlights and whites are easily achieved with a sharpened matchstick or toothpick, and the finger wrapped in a bit of rag gives another effect.

Using the same principle as in drawing with other media, the direction of the lines and textures will enhance the form and mood, such as in modeling around the contours of a face or figure, or in the horizontal brush strokes across the ground plane of a landscape.

The borders of the design can be cleaned of surplus ink with a ruler and a clean rag when work is completed, after which it is ready for printing.

Now lift out of the water the paper which has been soaking and drain off the excess moisture by holding the paper up by two of the corners. When this has been done, place it between several sheets of clean newsprint or white blotting paper and press gently

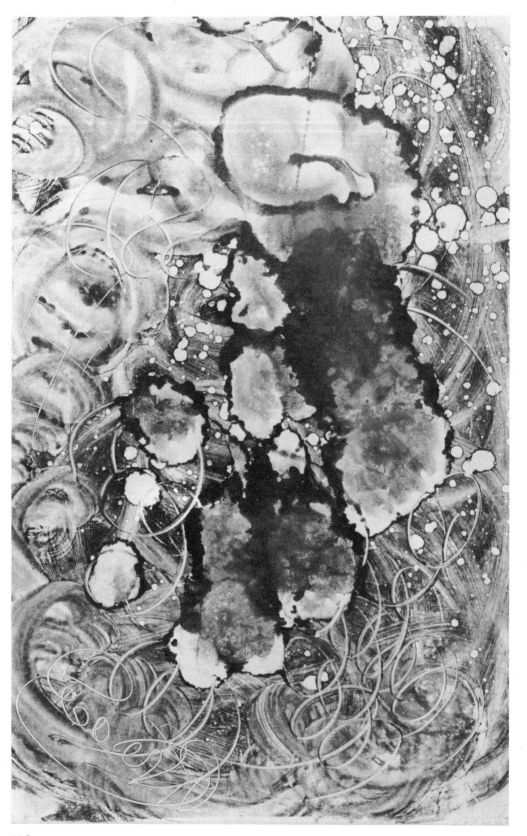

112

To protect against the printing paper slipping, and to secure it while it is lifted up to see how the transfer is proceeding, one edge may be taped to the plate, to act as a hinge.

until all surplus water is out of the paper or until it is limp and mat, without any gloss. Etching blotters are of the finest quality for serious work. If a type of printing paper is being used that requires only a little dampening, it can be done by placing it between dampened blotting paper, eliminating the preliminary soaking. This should be done especially with fragile Oriental papers and others that cannot stand much soaking.

Carefully lay the paper on the plate in one movement so as not to smear the ink. If the rubbing is to be done by hand, hinge the top edge of the paper to the plate with masking tape to ensure its not slipping, and so that it will return to its original position after being lifted up for examining the progress of the transfer. Place a sheet of newsprint on top of the printing paper before beginning the rubbing.

The physical effort necessary to make the transfer is much greater with stiff ink or paint. A hard-surfaced tool is required, either a steel roller or the back of the bowl of a tablespoon rubbed across the reverse side of the paper. Although doing it with a spoon involves more time and work, it has an advantage over the roller in that, because of the varying thickness of ink on the plate, an uneven pressure is sometimes necessary to make the impression.

For certain textural and tonal effects,

Pool Bottom. Monotype by Rea Treacy. A thin coat of stiff printers' ink was first applied and textured with a large, stiff brush and a pointed stick. Certain areas were then softened with a sable brush dipped in thinner. Finally, drops of thinner were flipped onto the surface, achieving the contrasting patterns seen in the center of the design.

Aaron Burr's Grave. Monotype by Gwyneth King Brown. In this print, pressures of the spoon were varied in the rubbing, certain areas being deliberately missed in order to obtain pure whites.

Collection, Firestone Library, Princeton University.

Snow Storm. Monotype by Gwyneth King Brown. Here the artist has employed the back of the bowl of a spoon to transfer the design, taking advantage of the process to depict the wind-blown snow and other elements. By varying the pressure and controlling the movements of the hand, the creative process is carried on in the printing, as well as in the painting of the picture.

Collection, Firestone Library, Princeton University.

the correct rubbing is as important as the method of applying the ink. The monotypist who is interested in producing first-rate prints will perfect every detail of the different phases of designing, painting, and printing.

Second prints are seldom possible with a stiff ink, unless the first one fails to transfer at all.

When using an etching press or wringer, follow the same procedure as described for the additive method, with the exception that with a stiff ink, greater pressure is required.

ADDITIVE METHOD

There are two widely different effects that can be obtained with the additive method, one by using fairly thick pigment, and the other with the consistency quite thin. Each of these approaches ordinarily requires a different type of paper and somewhat different handling in making the impression. The thick-pigment technique is the more predictable and is closer to that of oil painting, so we shall outline it first as an example of the additive method.

After completing the sketch of the subject to be carried out, place it face up underneath the transparent plate so that it can be followed in working out the painting.

If it is felt that a detailed sketch is not necessary, block out the design directly on the glass with a lithographic crayon, then turn over the plate, leaving the drawing on the underside. In this case place a piece of white or light-toned paper under the plate so that the lines will show up well, and as a background for working out the painting.

One of the advantages of making the sketch directly on the glass in this way is that when it is turned over it will be reversed, then when the impression is made it will be changed back again to the way it was originally designed on the plate.

While the paper is soaking, begin painting the design on the plate. In a manner similar to painting a picture on canvas, be direct and with as little working over as possible, for this will show up as muddiness in the final print. It is preferable to have the correct color mixed before placing it onto the plate, wherever possible. When the impression is made, two colors painted one over the other have a tendency to merge into one, as though they had been pre-mixed. Take this into account when painting the picture.

It is better to let the light paper show through for the highlights or lighter-toned areas, rather than to add white or light color. As a general rule, with the additive method, start with the lighter areas and work toward the darker ones. In doing this, you achieve any modeling of form by adding to the paint thickness as the dark areas are approached, in contrast to the thinner, lighter ones.

Text continued on page 120   115

The author's wife, Bettie, illustrates how to make an additive monotype. It will be seen that this approach is almost exactly the same as in making an oil painting on canvas, except that here it is painted on a glass plate and transferred to paper.

3. After the work is completed, a sheet of dampened paper is laid over the painting.

1. A sketch is made the same size as the monotype will be.

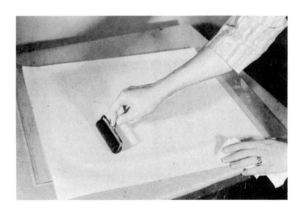

4. The back is rubbed with a spoon or hard roller, transferring the paint from the glass to the paper.

2. The sketch is placed under the transparent plate and, following the outlines, the picture is painted on the glass.

5. The print is pulled.

6. The result: "Rooster."

Night Blooming Cereus by Paul Rohland. A photograph of the actual paint residue left on the glass plate after a print has been pulled, showing how much paint was considered necessary for achieving the particular results wanted by this artist.

Roses. Monotype by Paul Rohland. Oil paint thinned with kerosene, printed on absorbent Japanese paper. Painted mainly with a stiff bristle brush, with occasional markings of a sharpened match stick for delineation.

Collection, Caroline Rohland, Bearsville, New York.

With a little practice, you will be able to tell how dense the paint should be in the dark areas and how meager in the light ones. Too much paint may spread, and too little may not show up in making the impression. Generally, the novice tends to apply paint too heavily.

Another thing to keep in mind is the relation of light–dark values in the painting, compared to the way they will appear on the print. Ordinarily, colors turn out darker in the printing than they seem to be on the plate.

If a slight amount of slow-drying oil (poppy oil) is added to the paints, there is no need to rush through with the painting for fear that it will dry before it is printed. In the event that the picture cannot be completed in one sitting, keep the paint in a soluble state for a day or two by placing the plate under water.

In adding oils of any kind to the paint or ink, remember that this will change the consistency so that it works differently than if it were stiffer. Some artists prefer this. This and other ideas are given as possible variations to be used when or if it happens to fit the particular problem at hand.

When using fast-drying paints or inks it is not always possible to complete the whole picture before the pigment dries. In this case, depending on the style, of course, small sections can be painted and printed before going on to others. Be sure to place the paper

in the correct position each time by the use of register marks on the plate, or by securing the top edge with masking tape.

While being careful not to smudge the painting on the plate by touching with the hands or by moving the paper after it has once touched the paint, place the damp paper on the design; then, working from the center outward, smooth the paper until it is flat on the plate.

At this point it is well to indicate with a lithographic crayon or glue tape where the corners of the paper are on the plate, as register marks in the event that it may be necessary to replace the paper in the same position for any retouching or overlay printing after the first impression is made.

Using a hard rubber brayer, the back of the bowl of a spoon or the hand, rub over the back of the paper until the paint is transferred from the plate. When thin paper is used, another sheet of paper should be placed over it before rubbing, to protect the thin sheet from tearing. Wax paper is good for this. It is all right to pull up an edge of the paper to see how the transfer is progressing, but take care not to move the paper out of position. It is wise to hinge the top edge of the paper to the plate with masking tape before starting the rubbing, to ensure that it does not slip.

If the printing is going to be done on an etching press or clothes wringer instead of being rubbed by hand, the following procedure is recommended: Before placing the damp paper on the plate, cut two pieces of poster board or similar weight cardboard a little larger than the size of the plate.

Hinge these together at one end with glue tape and open out flat on a desk or table. On one half, place two or three sheets of blotting paper for padding, then laying the plate on top of it, carefully place the printing paper on this and smooth it out.

On top of the paper, place some more blotters for padding, fold the second half of the cardboard over the top and run it through the press, with the closed end of the cardboard first. Sometimes it is desirable to run the plate back and forth in the press a few times to get the desired strength in the impression.

In using a mechanical press, the pressure must be right to ensure a good print. Too much pressure will squeeze the paint off the plate; too little will not obtain a strong enough impression. Never rest the rollers on the backing of the paper. In order to equalize the pressure, place a flat piece of plywood or fiberboard on top of the padded plate before printing. A few preliminary tests for pressure and correct amount of paint may save spoiling a serious attempt.

Upon completing the printing, pull off the paper and examine the finished results. If certain areas need retouching, it is usually more acceptable to do this on the plate; then replace the print on

For touching up, or for overlay printing, register marks are made on the plate with lithographic crayon or masking tape. This ensures that in all subsequent printings the paper will be replaced in exactly the same position. The marks are made by drawing a cross at each corner of the paper.

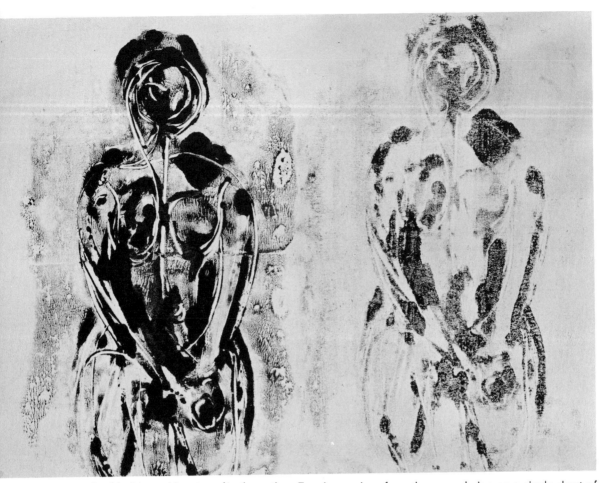

Double Image. Monotype by the author. Two impressions from the same design on a single sheet of paper, illustrating the differences between a first and second print.

the register marks, and run it through the press again. Another way to retouch is to do it on the print, then replace it on the clean plate, and run it through the press so that the retouched areas will acquire the same texture and appearance as the rest of the print.

Some artists are not against retouching or working directly on the print after the impression is made, while others take a more puristic view, feeling that there is something dishonest about doing this, or in fact about doing any retouching at all.

Sometimes it is possible to run a second print from the remaining paint on the plate. In fact, sometimes a second or third print is more interesting than the first. At first thought, this would seem to be breaking the rule that a monotype must be one of a kind, but actually it is impossible to obtain two prints exactly alike, even when they are pulled from the same plate, for whatever pigment remains after the first impression, it will produce a much lighter and entirely different effect than the first one.

In the event that a first print is unsatisfactory, or even if it turns out all right and you wish to use the remaining paint on the plate as a beginning for another print, more paint can be added to complete another design.

If a metal plate is used, it is sometimes possible to obtain a second print by slightly heating the back of the plate until the pigment becomes soft and then running it through the press.

When dampened paper is used, tack the finished print to a board until dry, or if a paper is used that tends to warp or buckle, place it between a couple of pieces of blotter or other absorbent paper and put a weight on top if it until it is dry. To hasten the drying and to be sure that the paint is fixed, you can place the paper aside for a short time until it is about three-fourths dry, then place it under the weight.

Finished prints can be better judged for quality when matted. The artist might keep several mats of various sizes and proportions on hand, so that as soon as the print is pulled it can be placed in one of these for studying the final result.

Prints done on transparent papers show up to better advantage when mounted if they are backed with white or light paper. The character of a print on such paper can be changed by using one of several colored papers in the backing.

The subtractive can be combined with the thick pigment additive technique, where more emphasis is placed on color. This is done by first more or less completing the painting in full color on the plate in the usual way, then with a stiff brush, cotton pads, and wooden sticks, subtracting some of the paint from the plate for high lights, lineal accents, or textures.

THIN PIGMENT METHOD

The use of thin pigment on the plate also can be said to come within the additive process, but the results are quite different than when the paint is thicker.

For sheer creative fun and surprises, this is the most exciting of all the monotype processes. The results are similar to those achieved in the game of pressing ink blots between two sheets of paper to create imaginative designs and patterns, the difference here being that the monotype will be in color, and the artist has more to say about the subject matter, the design, and, by imposing a certain amount of control, it may be guided in a general way toward the final result. This thin pigment method and controlled use of the accidental is the author's main contribution to the development of the monotype.

By tightening or loosening his control over the medium by changing the consistency of the paint from thin to thicker, along with choosing a particular type of paper for the printing, the artist can obtain a wide choice of effects.

Aside from using the pigment in a moister state, there are few differences in the procedures used in the production of this kind of monotype from

123

those that were used for the kind with thick paint. As for the printing, with the more soluble paint, very little pressure is needed to make the transfer, so that it is better done by hand than on a mechanical press. The best method is to use a cloth pad for rubbing the back of the paper, so that any pigment that is squeezed out can be readily wiped up.

There are two ways of making paint more soluble, each producing a somewhat different effect: (*a*) Thinning the pigment on the palette and applying it directly onto the plate; or (*b*) after painting on glass with fairly heavy pigment, letting it dry out slightly, then spraying thinner onto this with an atomizer, or by filling a bristle brush

The Return of Ulysses. Pen and ink drawing over ink blots by Salvador Dali.

Collection, William S. Lieberman, New York.

Totem and Tabu. Oil painting by Max Ernst. Effects like these can be produced by starting with an all-over pattern of monotype textures obtained by using thin pigment, then after this dries, painting out some areas and developing others in an imaginative way.

William Copley Collection, Los Angeles County Museum.

with thinner and flipping it on. (The same results can be obtained by flipping some thinner onto paint remaining on the plate after printing a thick-pigment monotype.)

Slick papers take thin oil paints well, and work better without dampening with water. Papers that are more absorbent usually work better when dampened. The artist often can discover new kinds of papers by talking with some professional printer or lithographer. People of such technical trades know many tricks the monotypist could use, and they are usually very helpful and generous with their knowledge.

Papers can be surfaced to suit one's self without too much trouble. Most good books on the technique of painting will give details on how this is done.

Prints made from moist colors are often incomplete in the first impression, but by bringing out certain parts and accenting or adding where needed with a second, overlay impression, they can

Text continued on page 132

Turbulent Forest. Oil painting by Carl Morris. Varied surface textures obtained by using an indirect, offset approach.

Room of Contemporary Art, Albright Art Gallery, Buffalo.

Young Pine Forest in Bloom. Tempera painting on Oriental paper by Morris Graves. Transfer effects are often seen in the backgrounds of this artist's pictures.

Phillips Collection, Washington, D. C.

Saint and Tapir. Oil painting by Kelly Fearing.

Collection, Mrs. Wilson Schoellkopf, Dallas. Photograph, courtesy Valley House, Dallas.

Saint Rose of Lima. Oil painting by Kelly Fearing.

Collection, Webster Atkin, New York. Photograph, courtesy Valley House, Dallas.

Offset methods were used in both of the paintings on this page. These effects can be seen in the rock formations and in the traceries of the plants and shrubs, the backgrounds in both pictures distinguished by a kind of organic inevitability.

Making a monotype with crepe paper. A method useful for background texturing or for finished abstract or non-figurative prints.

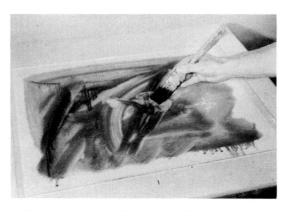

1. The background color is painted on the plate.

3. The wet crepe is placed on the plate and arranged for the particular design desired.

2. Crepe paper is soaked in paint thinned with turpentine.

4. Printing paper is laid over the crepe and the back of the paper is rubbed with a cloth.

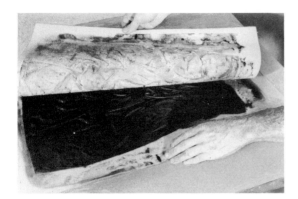

5. The print is pulled.

"Thicket." An abstract crepe print by the author.

Earl Minar shows how to make a mono-type with paper stencils.

3. The rough side of a piece of masonite is used for a plate. It is given a coat of printers' ink with a soft, gelatin brayer.

1. The design is drawn on stencil paper.

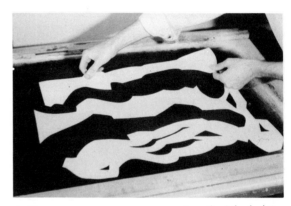

4. The paper cutouts are arranged on the inked plate.

2. The shapes are cut out with a mat knife.

5. Dampened rice paper is laid over the stencils.

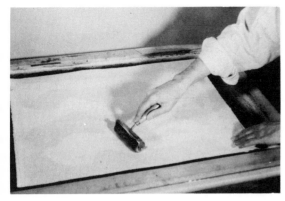

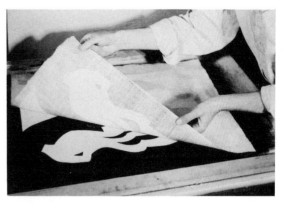

6. The back of the paper is rolled with a hard rubber brayer.

7. The print is pulled. Notice how the stencils have blocked out parts of the design.

Resulting print, showing textures which were transferred from the rough side of the masonite.

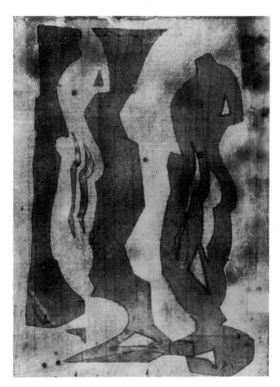

A second print by Earl Minar made by inking the paper cutouts and leaving the background blank, reversing the procedure used in the first print, seen on the preceding page.

sometimes be turned into very successful works.

The incomplete print can be studied for improvements, taking into account every accidental blot, daub, streak, or line, turning them to advantage in the second impression. For doing this, place the incomplete print under the transparent plate and use as a guide for blocking in the overlay design with lithographic crayon, then turn it over and follow the lines in the painting.

By consciously planning to achieve the final result in one or more overlay printings at the outset of work on the design, the chances of success are greater. Doing it this way, each part becomes more meaningful, and the whole work shows more clarity and directness.

This same procedure works well in conjunction with other media; for instance the first impression being done in moist oil paints and the second one with accents and lines using some type of oily mimeograph or labeling ink.

Great fun can be had by putting some moist paint on the plate in a more or less happenstance way, making an impression of it, then studying the results for possible development into a finished work. Depending on the particular imagination of the person doing it, faces, animals, landscapes, and other imaginary forms will suggest themselves for accenting and drawing out with subsequent printings, or for working on directly.

In the thin pigment method the artist finds wide, uncharted territory, oppor-

132

Text continued on page 140

Number 20, 1949. Oil painting by Boris Margo. A cello-monoprint was first made on the canvas, then it was painted over with oils.

1. Piece of paper to be used for printing is placed on plate and register marks drawn.

Steps in making an overlay monotype.

2. Design is drawn on glass plate with lithographic pencil.

4. Printing paper is placed on painted design, according to register marks.

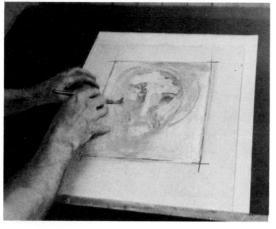

3. Plate is turned over and, following outline on underside of plate, middle tones are blocked in.

5. Pressure is applied to back of paper to obtain transfer of paint.

6. Paper is pulled, completing first printing.

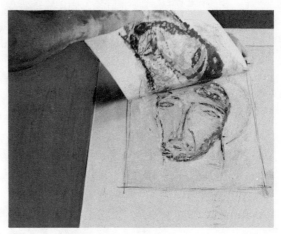

8. Carefully placing paper on plate again with use of the register marks, second printing is made and pulled.

7. After studying result and following the outlines on the underside of the plate again, dark ink or paint is applied for overlay printing.

9. Cardboard mat is placed over print for study of result.

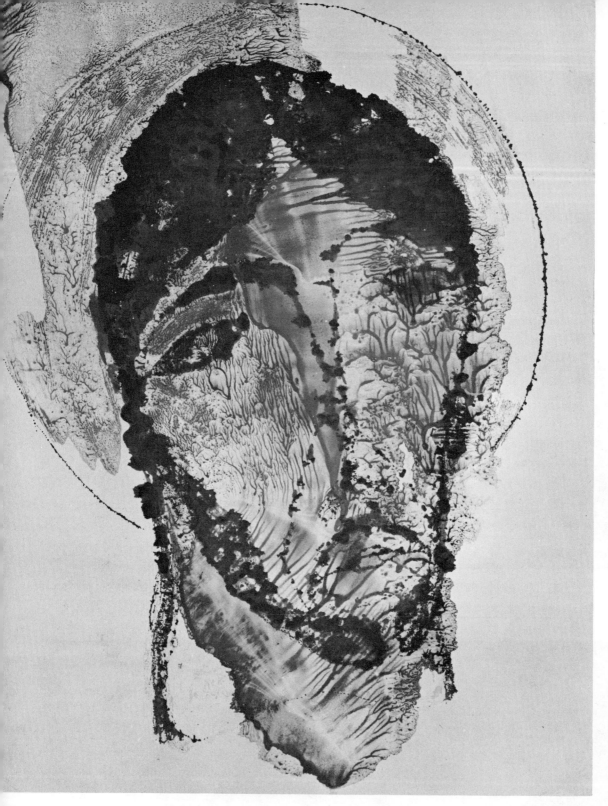

Head of Christ, 1948. Overlay monotype by the author. Thin pigment was used here, the downward running paint adding to the emotional quality of the subject.

Fishermen. Monoprint by Howard Schleeter.

The original prints by Schleeter are exceptionally rich in color and surface treatment, due to overlay printing. Here, black lines were first made by transfer drawing. Over these were printed transparent oil colors combined with printing inks. In some places color was added with the use of rubber cutouts and gelatin brayers of various sizes.

Petroglyphs. Monoprint by Howard Schleeter.

Animal, Inclosed Souls. Monoprint by Howard Schleeter.

Brayer painting.

1. Paint is spread on a flat surface and a thin film is picked up on the brayer.

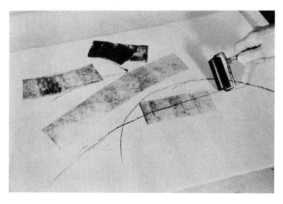

2. Ribbon-like patterns are made by rolling the brayer flat on the paper. Lines are obtained by using the edge of the brayer.

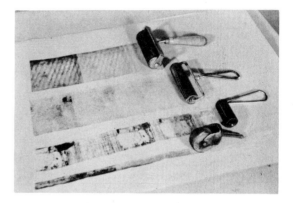

3. Brayers of various kinds and sizes create different effects.

4. Pitchers, 1952. Duco on masonite by the author. Painted entirely with brayers.

Collection, Mr. and Mrs. Carroll Barnes, Three Rivers, California.

Cans wrapped with string ready for printmaking.

tunity for excursions into the realm of "chance" or the "accidental." Some of the artists of earlier periods were aware of the importance or usefulness of the accidental, either as a point of imaginative departure, or as a means of obtaining finished results.

Vasari relates that Piero di Cosimo sometimes sat plunged in contemplation of a wall upon which certain sick persons had formed the habit of spitting. Out of these stains he created equestrian battles, fantastic towns, and the most magnificent landscapes. He did the same with the clouds and the sky.

In Leonardo's *Treatise on Painting,* he wrote, "It is not to be despised in my opinion, if, after gazing fixedly at a spot on the wall, the coals in a grate, the clouds, the flowing stream, if one remembers some of their aspects; and if you look at them carefully you will discover some quite admirable inventions. Of these the genius of the painter may take full advantage, to compose battles of animals and of men, of landscapes or monsters, of devils and other fantastic things which bring you honor."

If one is disposed, as many contemporary artists are, to eliminate natural or abstract likenesses from his vocabulary, the thin pigment method is a marvelous means of creating new and imaginative nonfigurative forms by controlling the laws of chance, or of cause and effect.

Certain surrealist painters, among

140

A group of can paintings by children of the Mt. Calvary Lutheran School, Omaha, Benjamin Marxhausen, instructor. In some of the examples shown, colored crayons were used to complete the design.

them Max Ernst and Salvador Dali have used similar methods for easel paintings, first letting the paint dry, after which imaginary figures and objects are developed from embryonic impressions, with certain areas being painted out to suggest sky and other background spaces. The original paint application may be done on a surface such as oilcloth and transferred to the canvas or panel, or done directly on the canvas in moist colors, after which oilcloth or paper is laid over it and pulled off to obtain suggestive forms and textures.

For either canvas or paper, a variation of this is obtained by dispensing with the glass plate, and laying a piece of cloth or white crepe paper on top of the canvas or printing paper, then laying a wash of thin oils or watercolor over it. The paint will seep through the crepe or cloth, after which it is pulled off, leaving a variety of sentient surfaces for further development into a picture, or as a textured background on which to paint.

An alternate use of crepe paper is to saturate it with thin paint before laying it on the plate, then placing printing paper on top of it and obtaining an impression by rubbing the back in the usual manner.

Another procedure for using paper is that of cutting stencils and using these to block out parts of the background in the printing.

OVERLAY PRINTING

Rich and beautiful effects can be achieved by superimposing one or more color impressions over another in subsequent printings. This is a technique that requires planning and skill, and is one for the advanced artist, rather than for the amateur or novice. Certain artists using this multiple impression method make as many as fifteen or twenty overlays on one picture to obtain the desired effect of color depth and luminosity.

A multiple impression monotype is created in ways similar to overlay glazing in easel painting. Working usually from light to dark, thin and more or less transparent color glazes are superimposed one by one, to arrive at the desired result.

Each preceding layer of paint or ink must be of the correct state of dryness before adding another, and the right proportion of pigment and extender or drier used in the mixture. All in all, the artist must become fairly skilled in the correct timing and other factors.

This need not frighten the novice away from attempting the use of overlay processes altogether, however, for the principle is a useful one and not altogether impossible for the beginner if it is kept simple, with not too many overlays used in the beginning.

Lithographic, printing, and etching inks are transparent and fine for over-

Charles Smith Makes a Blockpainting.

1. The appropriate block shapes are selected for the composition.

4. The block is placed in its proper position in the composition.

2. The background color is usually printed first with a large block.

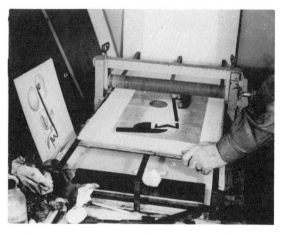

5. Pressure is applied to the block, transferring the color to the paper.

3. The color is then applied directly to the surface of the block.

6. The block is removed, others selected to complete the composition.

Moving Around. Blockpainting by Charles Smith.

Figure Composition. Blockpainting by Charles Smith.

Saint Paul. Woodblock-monotype by Paul Rohland. After printing, the excess paint was removed and another version made, but completely different in color.

Collection, Caroline Rohland, Bearsville, New York

lay work, or oil paints can be used by adding a little stand oil or clear varnish to give them more stiffness and traction when reduced to a thin glaze. A few drops of turpentine added to the glaze will thin it enough to keep it from becoming too sticky and drying too readily.

A heavy paper usually is required for multiple printing, something like heavy watercolor paper, illustration board, or the like.

CYLINDER TRANSFER

In the lithographic and printing trades the offset process often is used, wherein an image is picked up on a roller from a stone or plate and then transferred to paper. This same principle can be used successfully by the artist in painting, as well as in printmaking. Attractively textured backgrounds may be created by mixing some color on the plate, running the brayer

Text continued on page 149   145

Bird in Flight. Blockprint-monotype by Robert McLaren.

The Bullfight. Blockprint-monotype by Robert McLaren.

Wild Horses. Blockprint by Robert McLaren. While this print is almost outside the monotype field, it should be of interest to monotypists because of the unique way in which it was printed. An unincised piece of linoleum was given an all-over coat of ink and placed face up on the bed of an old George Washington hand press. On top of this was placed a piece of printing paper, and on top of the paper was laid face down a cut of the subject made from heavy cardboard. Pressure was then applied with the hand press, transferring the design to the underside of the paper.

This and other works by this artist reproduced here were printed from "blocks" made by incising double-weight matboard with a small X-acto knife. The color was applied with a brush and printed on black matboard, the pressure being applied by hand.

Now Flowing II. Relief print (26"x71" scroll) by Worden Day. Three widely varying impressions were made of the design. A watercolor sketch was first made on heavy tracing paper the same size as a piece of fiberboard to be used as a printing "block." Using yellow carbon paper so that it would show up well on the dark board, the outline of the sketch was traced. The lines were then carved into the panel, using a single-edged razor blade. After this, about eight coats of casein gesso were applied, the back of the panel being given the same number of coats to prevent warping. The brush was used to create textures, other effects were produced by building up the thickness of the gesso by controlled pouring, in the last two coats. Once thoroughly dry, the entire face of the panel was varnished and dried before the inking, to make it nonabsorbent. Oil paints combined with a transparent base were used for the printing, using gelatin rollers for the larger areas and various sizes of foam rubber rollers for the smaller ones.

Now Flowing III. Color Woodcut by Worden Day. This is not a monotype but the method used could easily be adapted by monotypists. The key block was a "found piece" (a grained piece of wood as found in nature) and the rest of the design was developed from this in subsequent overlays.

Softly-Softly. Blockprint-monotype by Franklin C. Watkins.

Collection, Philadelphia Museum of Art.

across it, then transferring it from the roller onto paper or canvas.

Natural surfaces of wood, cloth, wire screen, stone, linoleum, sandpaper, and other textures can be inked and transferred to canvas or other material.

The author has made extensive use of the roller-transfer technique for painting on fiberboard panels with oil paints and with synthetic enamels.

Brayer painting also can be done on paper, some glossy type being the most efficient, using printing inks of various colors.

When painting on fiberboard or canvas, it is better to start with less ink in the undertones, gradually adding heavier amounts as the work progresses. This also applies to the way in which colors and tones are developed, doing the lighter tints and shades first, leaving the heavier accents and stronger colors to the last.

Equinox. Color Etching with monotype methods used in the inking, by Rudy Pozzatti.

Text continued on page 153

149

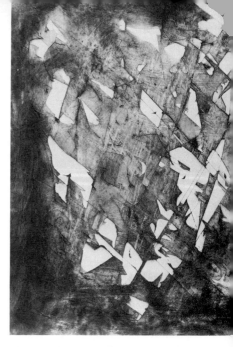

Print No. 1. Descendo. Printed in black.

Print No. 2. Arrival. Printed with stencils in three colors. Edition of ten variant prints in combination of mauve and orange. Experiments continued until plate cracked. It was then mended by Ibram Lassaw.

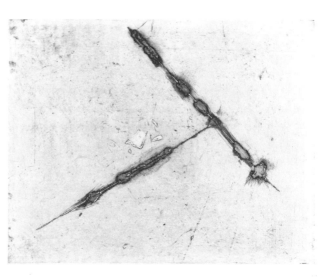

Print No. 3. Jet. Edition of two prints, one black, one venetian red — printed from back of plate, utilizing the mending material for achieving intaglio.

Print No. 4. Prehistoric Imagery. Printed from reverse of plate after having been cut in size. Edition of 15 variant prints in varying colors. Some prints torn by subsequent breaks in the mending had to be treated as colláges. Continued experiments on plate produced an interesting contrapuntal design to the jet pattern. Because of the precarious condition of the plate, decision was made to transfer both designs to a new plate.

Minna Citron's series of prints known as "The Uncharted Course" is a notable running example of an experimental, creative mind at work. Two of the prints might legitimately be called monotypes or monoprints, as only a single print was made of each. The others are etchings, although only a few prints were pulled in each case, and even here, most of the results are variable. This is the story of "The Uncharted Course" in the artist's own words: "I have been interested in the creative use of random or 'accidental' elements — which is perhaps another way of describing the relation between spontaneity and control. This interest was brought to focus by my experience with a plate which went through a number of interesting 'accidents,' all of which were successively developed in a series of prints. First, I noticed that an unusual pattern was formed when I began to take off its cellophane wrapper, and I 'helped out' this pattern by further 'intentional' tearing and cutting while the plate was in the acid bath. At that stage, I made a number of prints in black and white as well as in color, experimenting with a variety of stencils. Through overwork, the plate, which was very deeply engraved, broke in several places and my friend, Ibram Lassaw, was kind enough to mend it for me. The pattern of solder on the back was so attractive that I made several prints from the reverse side; the plate was then cut to a smaller format. More prints were made; the plate again broke and was once more mended. Soon the plate became impossible to use, so I transferred the design to a new plate which, when completed, became 'Slipstream.' "

Of two existent series of "The Uncharted Course," one was recently purchased and given to the New York Public Library by John Turner, New York.

Print No. 5. (Etát). Monoprint.

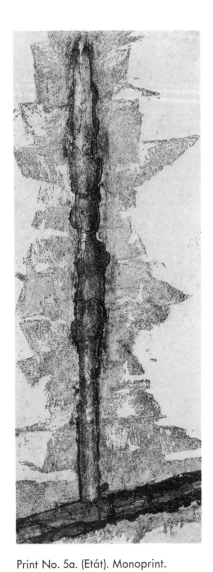

Print No. 5a. (Etát). Monoprint.

Print No. 6. Slipstream.

Photo-Monotype #6 by Frank Mulvey. Made by placing sensitized photographic paper on an incised surface wetted with hypo solution, after which the paper was developed like a regular photographic print.

Take care not to let the brayer get too filled with ink as time goes on and the colors dry on it. Clean it with thinner at intervals while working.

Colors usually are rolled onto the paper or canvas one at a time, different colors and effects being produced by applying one over another.

Other cylindrical objects, such as rolling pins, bottles, and tin cans, make good tools for certain kinds of transfer prints and paintings.

Reinhold Marxhausen, an art in-structor, uses a method of tin can painting which he finds of creative interest to art students, a procedure that might be adapted by the more advanced student or professional. It should be of special interest to the designer of fabrics, wallpaper, packaging and the like.

The following pointers are contributed by him for those interested in experimenting with the idea:

1. Cut off the bottom and top of a tin can, including the rim. A cylinder of tin remains.

2. Paint the outside of the cylinder with Elmer's glue.

3. Wrap a length of string around the outside in any way you choose. It may overlap a string of different size. Any size of loosely twisted string or yarn may be used. (If it is thick enough the rims need not be removed from the can.)

4. When the glue is thoroughly dry, paint the string with writing ink, India ink, thin tempera, or textile paint. The string serves as a reservoir and the metal cylinder will not absorb and waste the paint as would cardboard or wood.

5. Hold the can by putting the fingers inside it, then roll the ink onto cloth or paper. Apply only slight pressure at first. As the ink supply is depleted, more pressure is required.

6. When the ink is gone, stop the can with its seam at the bottom. At this point make a *T* mark with a pencil, one line along the edge of the can and the other intersecting at the position of the seam, and the design will carry through without a break.

The design may be printed in many different ways: vertically, horizontally, reversing the design in alternate rows, or overprinting with another color.

WOODBLOCK TRANSFER

Blocks of wood cut in various shapes and sizes can be arranged into a composition, ink rolled over them with a brayer, and then printed in a press.

154

Printers' inks and oil paints both work well with this type of printmaking, but are better when rolled out quite thin, and with little or no thinner added.

Another way of using woodblock patterns is to build the composition piece by piece, extemporizing as the work proceeds. Charles Smith, the foremost exponent of this method, uses a converted squeeze photo print drier for pulling the prints. The blocks he uses are type-high, so an ordinary etching press could not accommodate them.

This differs from the ordinary monotype procedure, in that instead of painting the whole picture on the plate and making one impression from this, the design is constructed gradually by successive printings of variously shaped blocks. A sketch of the design of the visualized work in completion may be followed, but not too rigidly. Allow leeway to adjust and rearrange as the picture takes form.

The rule that a true monotype must be printed all in one impression is broken here, so that it would perhaps be called a near-monotype process, but the truly creative artist is not too concerned with categories and labels, but rather with using any means that will enhance and broaden his expressive powers.

Paintings created directly on paper or canvas by transferring the pigment from blocks, cardboard cutouts, the points or edges of wooden sticks, metal strips and other objects, but without a press, have much of the finesse, textural

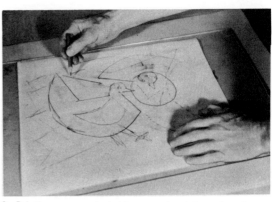

2. Printing paper is laid upon the ink and, using a pencil or pointed stick, the design is drawn on the back of the paper.

Steps in making a transfer drawing.

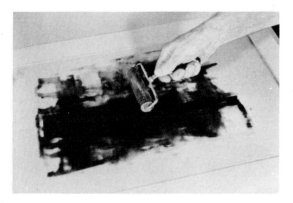

1. The plate is given an all-over coat of dark ink.

3. The print is pulled, the drawing having been transferred to the underside of the paper.

subtlety, and charm of a monotype print.

Working directly this way, there are no limits to the size of the picture possible, from a small painting on paper, up to an easel painting or a large mural.

BLOCKPRINT MONOTYPE

Blockprinting in the usual sense is done by cutting lines on a wood or linoleum block and then inking and printing. This art can be combined with monotype, certain lines being cut in the block as part of the design, to be used as a guide for producing more than one similar, but not exactly like, prints of a chosen subject.

Another monotype-blockprint method is to cut stencils and apply paint through these onto a wood or linoleum block, then after the stencil is removed, lay a piece of paper over the block and make a print in the traditional manner of producing a monotype. In this way, large numbers of similar prints can be made, while taking advantage of the surface effects possible in a transfer method.

Text continued on page 158   155

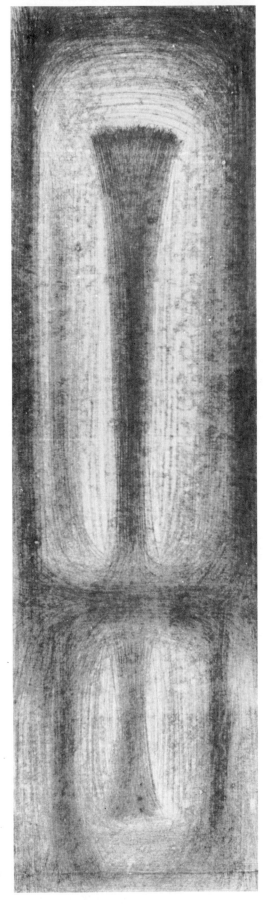

Untitled monoprints (transfer drawings) by Harry Bertoia. Made by spreading printers' ink on a table top, laying paper upon it and drawing the lines and smudges from the back of the paper, the sensitive degree of pressure producing the different tonal effects.

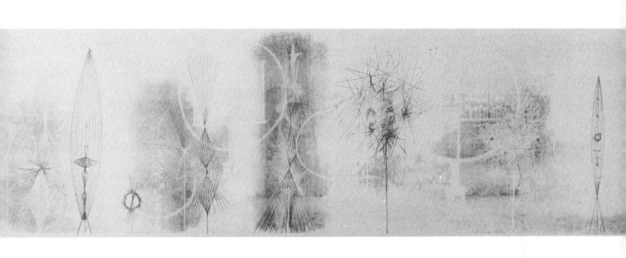

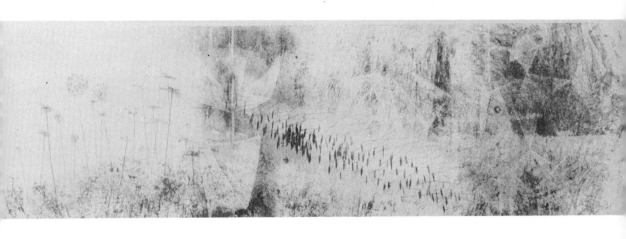

Timberline Tree. Watercolor-ink monotype by Dwight Kirsch. The action of the India ink-water mixture caused the interesting granulation seen on the tree limbs, producing effects quite different from those seen in oil base monotypes.

ETCHING MONOTYPE

Monotype procedures also can be combined with those of making etchings, parts of the design on the metal plate being etched in line, tone or texture, then the coloring applied freely before each print is run through the press.

On etching-monotype effects, the late American etcher, Joseph Pennell is recorded as saying, "There are many other forms of etching. One very interesting method is to take a plain copper plate and cover the face of it with a coating of ink, then proceed, by means of rags and paintbrushes and anything which comes handy, especially the fingers, to

158

Field Flowers, Yaddo. Sumi ink monotype by Dwight Kirsch. This was painted on a Plexiglas plate and transferred to a soft, variegated Japanese paper, producing a subtle, delicate quality.

Bebop Concert. Monogouache by Madeline Tourtelot. Black silk-screen paint was first applied with roller, scraper, and spatula and transferred to white charcoal paper. When dry, colors in soft tints were rolled directly over the print, sometimes with only slight pressure, in order to obtain transparent effects.

Loneliness. Monogouache by Madeline Tourtelot. A combination of monotype and direct over-painting with gouache. The first step was to work black silk-screen paint on a glass plate. This was offset onto a piece of gray charcoal paper. The thickness of the paint caused branchlike ridges, which when dry were brought out with direct painting, using white casein applied with the fingers. The final values were achieved by adding casein colors with a Chinese brush.

make a design on it, painting from dark to light.

"When the design is made it is passed through a press and the design comes off on the paper. I recall several Venetian etching studies by Whistler in which he freely varied the tones on the plates in this way."

PHOTOGRAPH MONOTYPE

The photo-monotype by Frank Mulvey on page 153 illustrates one of many possibilities for combining monotype with photography. In this instance a common chemical (hypo) solution was applied to the surfaces of a flat area, textured in low relief. An old drawing board which had been used for cutting picture mats, resulting in a pattern of incised lines, was used in the example shown.

With the room darkened, a sheet of sensitized print paper was pressed face down on the chemically treated surface. After removing the paper it was exposed to light. The ordinary process of photographic print development was then followed, resulting in a transfer

End of a Queen. Monotype printed over a watercolor background, with white lines added by using the edge of a wooden stick or palette knife. By Don Baum.

of textures similar to those on the drawing board.

Another way of making photo-monotypes is to cover a piece of transparent glass or plastic with stiff black ink, or paint stiffened with the addition of a little varnish, and then scratch or wipe out parts of it to make a design, after which it is used as a photographic negative and prints made from it. The Barbizon painters made many such prints.

162

CRAYON MONOTYPE

Transferring a crayon picture onto paper is somewhat of a different problem than with paint or ink. The surface of the plate needs to have a certain amount of tooth or texture to which the crayon will cling when it is drawn across it, such as in ground glass or fine sandpaper.

Hand-ground glass plates are better

Text continued on page 167

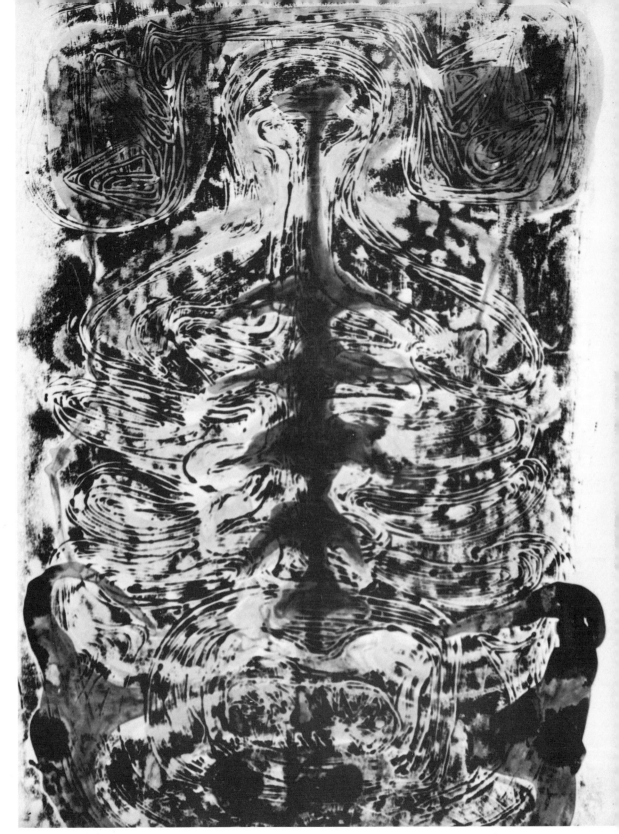

The Apparition. Monotype in printers' ink, over a watercolor background. In this unusual combination, Don Baum first painted parts of the picture directly onto paper with watercolors, on top of which the concluding part of the design was added with printers' ink transferred from a glass plate.

Example of preliminary patterns in water color-monotype, before working over with pastel.

An example of a mixed technique is that used by Roger Crossgrove, who combines monotype with pastel in an original manner. He uses a water-starch recipe like the one given for watercolor monotypes, adding this to designers' colors and working on a glass or plastic plate with a certain amount of tooth on the surface.

Starting with an arbitrary design similar to that shown here, he lets it dry thoroughly, studying it for possible development, and how it will combine with pastel.

By using a soft mulberry paper he is able to make transitions and adjacent areas in the two media completely indistinguishable from each other, thus making a good marriage of the two.

Working over the picture a great deal with pastel, it is sprayed at frequent intervals with Krylon or other fixitive. Just before it is framed and put under glass, the picture is given a last coat of pastel which is left dry and unfixed. This helps to retain the pure colors and special qualities of pastel in the work.

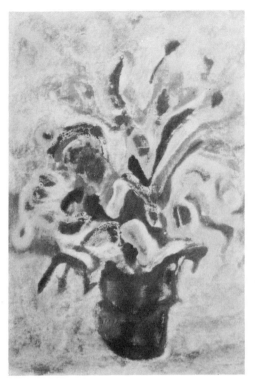

Bouquet of Flowers. Pastel painted over water-color-monotype, by Roger Crossgrove.

Imaginary Bouquet. Pastel painted over water-color-monotype, by Roger Crossgrove.

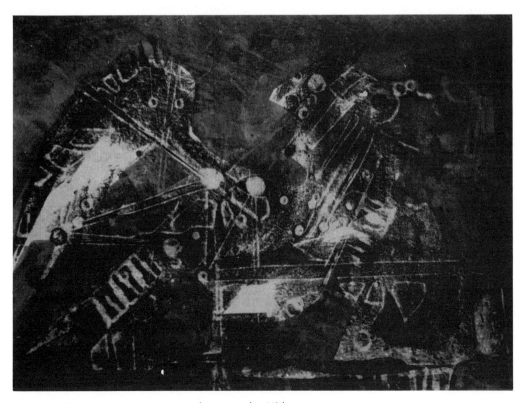

The Lion of San Marco. Monotype and tempera by Mirko.

The Meeting. Monotype by Mirko.

Chimera. Monotype and tempera by Mirko. A monotype was first printed, after which certain areas of the background were painted over with thin tempera.

than the commercial ones, which are often merely frosted imitations. A heavy piece of plate glass can be ground by hand, using the same grinding powders that the etcher uses in surfacing plates of zinc or copper. Carborundum powder #150 is a good one for this use.

From certain art supply or offset printers' supply stores one can purchase thin zinc plates in a variety of textures. These are made for use in offset lithography, but are excellent for crayon monotypes, and cost very little.

If sandpaper is used, the finest grades, such as 3/0, are best. This should be of the white variety, not the black, so that the crayon marks can be seen while the design is drawn.

The William Korns lithographic crayons are good for the drawing, and can be purchased at most places where art supplies are sold. They can be obtained in several grades, from soft to hard. The hard ones, such as #6, are used for the lighter and more delicate tones, and the softer ones, such as #3, are used for heavy darks and solid blacks.

The usual colored crayons are softer and waxier, and ordinarily do not make as good an impression as the lithographic ones, but the reader may find it an interesting experiment to try them.

Soft, absorbent papers are best for the prints. Instead of dampening the paper with water, dampen it with tur-

Sadness. Monopen by Enid Foster. Pen lines over monotype patterns.

pentine. Using a cloth or cotton pad, saturate the paper evenly and wipe up the excess so that no gloss remains. Carefully brush off all the excess bits of crayon particles from the plate or sandpaper before printing, so that these will not cause any displeasing blots on the finished print.

A mechanical press of some kind is best for the printing of crayon monotypes, because they cannot be transferred without fairly heavy pressures. Second choice would be a barin or the back of a spoon.

Lay the turpentine-dampened paper on the plate and place a piece of blotting paper over this for a blanket. Then place the two papers between two heavy pieces of hinged cardboard, and run the

whole arrangement through the wringer or etching press. Experiments will tell just how much pressure is necessary for best results.

A few extra pieces of blotting paper placed under and over the cardboards will ensure a better print when an etching press is used.

It is possible to use heat in transferring crayon monotypes. Make the drawing on a surfaced metal plate, and apply heat on the underside until the crayon is of the correct melted state. Then run it through the press.

Another way is to make a crayon drawing on paper, and after placing the printing paper over this, rub a hot flat-iron across it until the crayon is melted and picked up by the printing paper.

168

Text continued on page 172

Three steps in the creation of a monopen by Enid Foster.

1. With a painting knife, patches of paint are placed in a random manner on a smooth surface and transferred to paper.

2. After studying the suggestive shapes, faces and other forms are outlined with pen and ink.

3. Forms are further delineated and colors and textures added to complete the picture. The finished result is titled "Many Actresses Passing Through a Part."

Composition. Monoprint with additions in pencil and ink by John Wood. An example of a mixed technique.

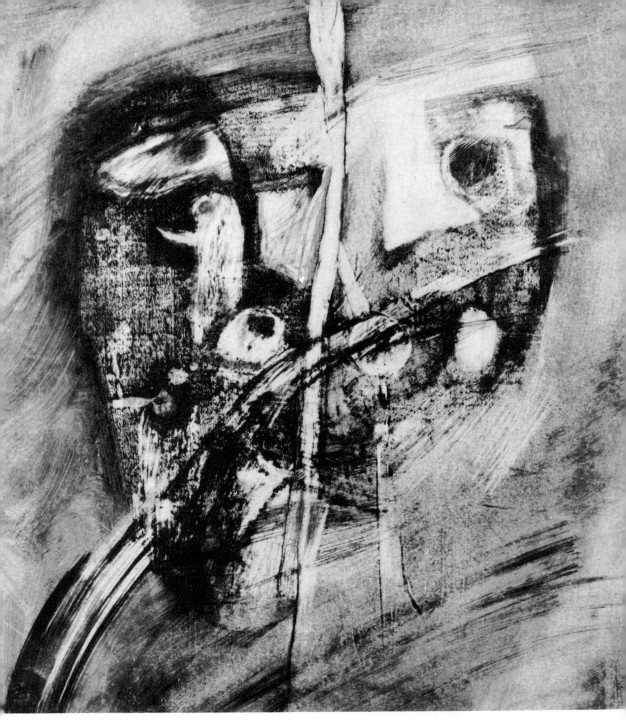

Head. Monoprint worked over with lithographic pencil by John Wood.

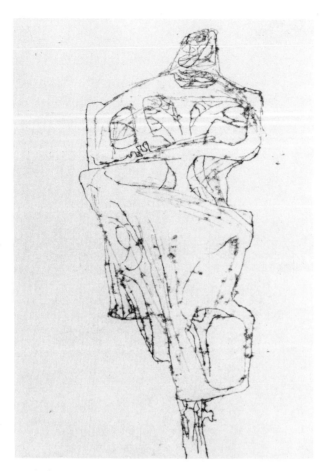

Study for ceramic sculpture. Monoprint by Daniel Rhodes.

The effect desired can be controlled to some extent by the degree of heat applied. Use this same system for transferring designs from paper onto cloth.

TRANSFER DRAWINGS

Beautiful lineal work can be achieved by rolling a coat of ink onto the plate, then laying the printing paper upon this and drawing on the back of the paper with a stylus or pointed stick, the lines being transferred in reverse on the underside of the paper as the drawing is done. A plate made of end grain maple serves better than glass for transfer drawings. The coat of ink and the weight of the paper must be so that the ink does not blot except as desired, and for some minor accidental effects.

By reversing the usual procedure of doing a black or dark line on light paper, and using white paint on black paper, some stunning effects are possible. Drawings in color also may be done in this manner.

By rubbing lightly with the fingers or a soft tool on the back of the paper in certain areas, tonal effects are obtainable, to combine with those of sharp line.

Make the original sketch on the same paper that is to be printed on. Then, keeping the drawing right side up, trace

Study for ceramic sculpture. Monoprint by Daniel Rhodes.

Among the many other uses of monotype, some artists find it a handy means of making sketches for easel paintings, murals, and sculpture.

Walter Rivers demonstrates how to make a painting from a monotype detail.

1. After making a monotype, a small aperture is cut from a piece of matboard in the proportions wanted.

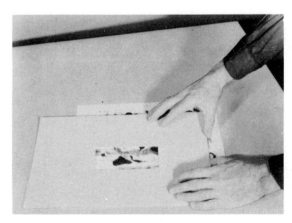

2. The mat is placed over various parts of the design to find the best composition.

the lines through; the paper will pick up the impression on the underside. Another way is to make the sketch on thin paper, lay this over the printing paper, and then trace over the lines.

WATERCOLOR MONOTYPE

Transparent watercolors are hard to control in making a monotype, because they do not have enough body to adhere to the plate. Thin oils can duplicate most of the effects that are possible

with transparent watercolors, and are much easier to handle. An opaque watercolor, such as gouache or water-base printing ink, usually contains enough filler to give it some body, and so comes nearer to being a workable medium.

Fingerpaints, either those sold commercially or the homemade variety, can be used for this type of work, although the permanency is questionable. However, this need not be a deterrent for school projects.

Starch paste is sometimes used as an

174

3. Several different possibilities are seen as the mat is moved about.

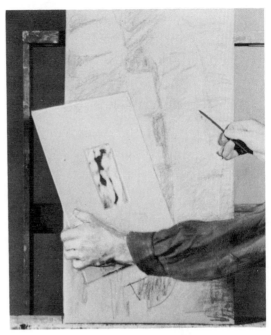

5. The composition is enlarged onto a panel of similar proportions.

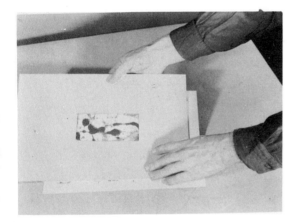

4. An area of the design is finally decided upon.

extender and binder for watercolor monotypes. The artist Dwight Kirsch contributes the following mixtures for adding to water-soluble paints and inks:

1. Boiled cornstarch or
   laundry starch: 3 parts
   Glycerin: 1 part
   Clear honey: 1 part

Stir or shake well until these ingredients are thoroughly mixed. If one wishes to keep a batch of the medium for more than a few days, add three or four drops of phenol (carbolic acid) to

Text continued on page 179

6. The sketch is put aside and the painting is developed and improved upon as it is carried toward completion.

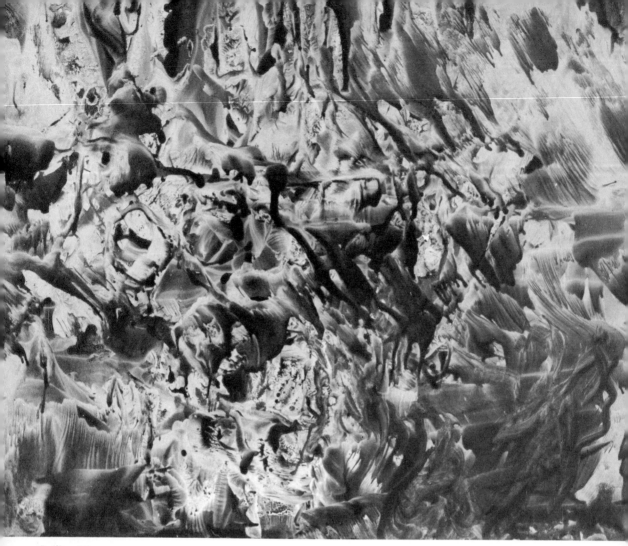

Boiling Microcosm.

Three examples of monopaintings by the author. They are done in difficult techniques which may be useful to the advanced artist. Using a very thin oil paint and glossy paper, the design and form were controlled in a different way for each work shown. The forms in "Landscape-Ascension" were achieved by first creasing the paper so that some areas did not pick up any pigment in the printing. "Midnight Rock" was made by embossing the paper with a blunt pointed stick before printing, thus deciding the way the paint adhered to the paper. "Boiling Microcosm" was produced by manipulating the paper on the plate covered with thin paint, and by several overlays while the print was still in a tacky state. No brushes or tools of any kind were used to draw the forms in these three examples, all the control and creative effort taking place in the preparation of the paper beforehand, and in the manipulation of the paper directly on the plate of thin pigment in the printing.

Landscape-Ascension.

Midnight Rock.

each pint of the medium. The starch should be thinner than that used for pudding or for starching laundry, about the consistency of thin jelly when cold. Cornstarch is finer textured and seems to stay moist longer than laundry starch.

Substitute Recipe

2. Boiled cornstarch: 3 parts
   Honey: 1 part
   Salad oil (Mazola
     or Wesson)   1 teaspoon to
                   each pint of
                   above mixture

Slowly add the oil, drop by drop, while beating the mixture. This substitute medium should be stirred or shaken before using. Add phenol for preservative, as in No. 1.

Starch medium is added to any kind of water-soluble paints as an extender and to prevent rapid drying when painting on a glass, plastic, or metal plate, before the paint is transferred to paper. Very little of the medium is required for tube watercolors, much more being needed for opaque ones, such as gouache or casein in tubes.

MIXED MEDIA

Just about any of the usual media that artists use can be combined with or applied over monotypes—lithography, woodblock, colored crayon, pastel, tempera, gouache, oils, water-soluble inks, and so on. Most of these can be used either as underpainting or overpaint-ing. There are few rules for this. Each artist will work out a means to fit his own particular expressive desires.

CONCLUSION

A number of monotype and related techniques have been outlined or suggested herein, and the reader is left with the happy task of trying them out, experimenting with them, and perfecting them for his own uses.

Nothing has been said about form, design, or style. It is taken for granted that the quality of any art work depends not only on the technical proficiency of the artist, but to a greater extent on the formal and expressive values he is able to project into the work. The serious student or artist will use any technical means such as those found in this book as an added means to an end, the end being a work of art complete in every aspect—design, color, form, technique, a creative, personal expression.*

It is hoped that the experienced monotypist may have had a few new doors opened to him. The author is sure that the novice has many fascinating experiences ahead in working with this medium, whether it is used as a loosening-up exercise for painting or printmaking, an adjunct to other processes, or as a full-fledged art in its own right.

*See *Art Structure*, a textbook of creative design, by Henry N. Rasmusen, McGraw-Hill Book Co., 1950.

BIBLIOGRAPHY *

DAS MONOTYPE, by S. R. Koehler. *Chronik für vervielfältigende Kunst.* Wein, 1891; Jahrg. 4, no. 3, p. 17-20.

ETCHING AND MEZZOTINT ENGRAVING. Lectures delivered at Oxford, by Sir Hubert Herkomer. The Macmillan Company, 1892; p. 104-107.

ETCHING, DRYPOINT, MEZZOTINT, by Hugh Paton. Raithby, Lawrence and Company, London, 1895.

A NEW BLACK AND WHITE ART. *The Studio,* Feb. 15, 1896; p. 30-36. An article on the monotypes of Sir Hubert Herkomer.

MONOTYPES. An article by Charles A. Coffin. *Century Magazine,* Feb., 1897; p. 517. "Coffin" is the pen name of the American printmaker, Charles A. Walker.

MONOTYPING, by Edward Ertz. *International Studio,* Sept., 1902; p. 170-175.

THE ART OF MONOTYPING. *International Studio,* 1904; vol. 23, p. 149-150.

MONOTYPES, by Christian Brinton. *Scribner's Magazine,* 1910; vol. 47, p. 509-512.

AMERICAN GRAPHIC ART, by Frank Weitenkampf. Henry Holt and Company, 1912; p. 133-136.

THE ENGRAVINGS OF WILLIAM BLAKE AND EDWARD CALVERT, by Lawrence Binyon. *Print Collectors Quarterly,* Dec., 1917.

CATALOG DES EAUX-FORTES, VERNIS-MOUS, AQUATINTS, LITHOGRAPHS AND MONOTYPES OF EDGAR DEGAS. PARIS, Nov., 1918. 139 monotypes listed, some illustrated.

PAUL DOUGHERTY'S MONOTYPES, by Frank Jewett Mather, Jr. *Vanity Fair Magazine,* 1919; vol. 12, p. 44.

*Titles are listed chronologically, and except where noted were published in the United States.

DELTEIL CATALOG. Paris, 1920. Describes three monotypes by Toulouse-Lautrec.

THE MONOTYPE, by Malo Renault. *Art and Decoration,* Paris, 1920; vol. 37, p. 49-56.

A CHINESE ALBUM. Eight monotype figure studies, by Cyrus Leroy. Baldridge. *Asia Magazine,* Dec., 1921.

THE MONOTYPES OF GIO. BENEDETTO CASTIGLIONE, by Augusto Calabi. *Print Collectors Quarterly,* Oct., 1923; Dec., 1925; July, 1930.

BYBLIS MAGAZINE, 1923. An article on monotypes.

THE ENGRAVED DESIGNS OF WILLIAM BLAKE AND EDWARD CALVERT, by Lawrence Binyon. Charles Scribner's Sons, 1926.

HOW TO APPRECIATE PRINTS, by Frank Weitenkampf. Charles Scribner's Sons, 1929.

A MONOTYPE BY JAMES NASMYTH. *Print Collectors Quarterly,* Jan., 1929.

MARCEL GUIOT CATALOG. Paris, 1930. Gives a detailed description of the method used by Paul Gauguin in his later years, in the making of monotypes.

MAKING A MONOTYPE, by Seth Hoffman. *Milwaukee Institute Bulletin,* Jan., 1931; vol. 4, p. 12.

THE MONOTYPES OF SETH HOFFMAN, by Lundi Gilbert. *Prints Magazine,* Jan., 1931; p. 28-35.

GEISER CATALOG. Paris. Describes nine monotypes by Pablo Picasso, through 1931.

PICASSO, Painter-Engraver, 1898-1931, by Bernhard Geiser. Berne, 1933. Pablo Picasso monotypes described and illustrated under numbers 248-257.

ON MONOTYPES, by Kenneth M. and Mary E. Ballantyne. *Art in New Zealand,* Wellington, 1935; vol. 7, p. 197-208.

PAUL GAUGUIN'S INTIMATE JOURNALS (Avant et Après). Originally published in a complete facsimile edition limited to 100 copies, by Kurt Wolff, Leipzig, 1918. Later translated by Van Wyck Brooks and published by Crown Publishers, 1936. Contains a number of drawings which are either monotypes or monotypes with pen and ink added.

MONOTYPES, by I. T. O'Keeffe. *Prints Magazine,* June, 1937; vol. 7, p. 258-267.

ON THE MAKING OF MONOTYPES, by Henry C. Cogle. *The Artist,* Sept., Oct., and Nov., 1937.

NOTES ON THE MONOTYPE, by George Nelson. *Pencil Points Magazine,* Dec., 1937.

MONOTYPES: WHAT THEY ARE AND HOW THEY ARE MADE. *Art Instruction Magazine,* May, 1938; p. 17.

Monotypes by Another Method, by William S. Rice. *Art Instruction Magazine,* July, 1938; p. 21.

The Monotype, by Yves Brayer. *A.B.C. Magazine,* 1939; vol. 15, p. 189-190.

Abstractions — Reproductions, by Charles Smith. Johnson Publishing Company, 1939. Limited edition of 300 copies. Twenty-seven original black and white, and six color plates, printed by the artist.

How to Make a Monotype, by Will Barnet. A motion picture produced in 1939 for Educational Films, Inc.

How to Make a Monotype, by M. Benke. *Design Magazine,* Jan., 1940; p. 27.

Sandpaper Monotypes, by W. S. Reed. *Design Magazine,* Mar., 1940; p. 14-15.

The How and Why of a Monotype, by Paul Warren Ashby. A four-page pamphlet published by the American Monotype Society, 1941.

The Artist's Handbook, by Ralph Mayer. The Viking Press, 1943; p. 457.

Degas a la Recherché de sa Technique, by Denis Rouart. Floury, Paris, 1945.

Monotypes of Henry Nordhausen, by Ernest Watson. *American Artist Magazine,* June, 1947; p. 16-21.

The Monotypes of Paul Bransom. *The American Artist,* Apr., 1948.

E. Degas Monotypes, by Denis Rouart. Quatre Chemins, Editart, Paris, 1948; Shoman Art Company, Distributors. Forty monotypes by Degas reproduced.

Notes on the Monotypes of Degas, by Marcel Guérin. *Amour de l'art;* vol. 5, p. 77-80.

An Unpublished Manuscript by Paul Gauguin. Bulletin of the City Art Museum of St. Louis, summer, 1949. Gauguin monotypes pasted on front and back covers.

Try Your Hand at Monotype; two unusual art projects for advanced amateurs. *Design,* Columbus, Ohio, Sept.-Oct., 1953; vol. 55, no. 1, p. 20-21.

The Drawings of G. B. Castiglione and Stefano Dela Bella, in the Collection of Her Majesty the Queen, at Windsor Castle, by Sir Anthony Blunt, 1954. Four monotypes by Castiglione reproduced.

Blot Painting, by Mary F. Merwin. *School Arts Magazine,* May, 1954; p. 37.

Brayer Painting, by Shepard Levine. *School Arts Magazine,* May, 1954; p. 38.

Picasso — Fifty-five Years of His Graphic Work, by Bernhard Geiser and Hans Bolliger. Harry N. Abrams, Inc., 1955.

Matisse — 50 Years of His Graphic Art, by William S. Leiberman. George Braziller, 1956. Thirteen Matisse monotypes reproduced.

Gauguin Drawings, by John Rewald. Thomas Yoseloff, 1958. Seventeen Gauguin monotypes illustrated.

Tin Can Painting, by Reinhold Marxhausen. *Arts and Activities Magazine,* Jan., 1958; p. 16-18.

The Magic of Monotyping, by Berne W. Biteman. *Arts and Activities Magazine,* April, 1958.

Finger Paint for Printmaking? by Octavia C. Waldo. *Arts and Activities Magazine,* Oct., 1958; p. 12-14.

INDEX

Abramofsky, Israel, 63
  monotypes, 80, 81
Accidental effects, 140
Acid, Carbolic, 175, 179
Additive method, 115, 123
Alexander, J. W., 18
American Monotype Society, 87
Apian, Adolph, 26
Aquatint, 3
Archterwald, 26
Art Club of New York, 17
Ashby, Paul, 87
Australian monotypists, 68–71
Author (See Rasmusen, Henry)

Baby oil, 98
Bacher, Otto, 18
  monotype, 20
Bachertype, 18
Bagley, Henry N., 59
  floatagraph, 62
Baldridge, Cyrus Leroy, 63
Barile, Xavier, 87
Barin, 101, 168
  how to make a, 100
Barnet, Will, 87
Basic materials summary, 102
Basinwerks paper, 101
Bauhaus, 42
Baum, Don, 66
  monotypes, 162, 163
Beal, Gifford
  monotype, 56
Bernstein, Theresa, 63–66
  monotype, 85
Bertoia, Harry, 50, 63
  monoprints, 157, 158
  prototype, 58
Bicknell, A. H., 18
Binders, 97, 98
  definition, 98
  starch, 175
Biteman, Berne, 60, 65
Blake, William, 15, 17
  monotypes, 17, 18
Blanket, 168
Blockpaintings, 50
Blockprint
  brayer, 99
  inks, 97
  monotype, 155
  papers, 101
  press, 99
  variations in impressions, 3
Blocks, 54
  linoleum, 155
  wood, 64, 155
Blotter, 101, 107, 111, 113, 121, 168
  etching, 113
Blum, Robert, 18
Boudal, Jean
  monotype, 77
Bransom, Paul, 63
  monotype, 67
Brayers, 101, 102
Broner, Robert, 50, 66
  texture prints, 94
Brown, Gwyneth King, 57, 63
  monotypes, 114
Brushes, 99, 102, 111, 123
Buffer, 107
Bunce, Louis, 87

Cadard, 28
Calabi, Augusto, 14
Cameo paper, 101
Carborundum powder, 167
Cardboard, 99
  cutouts, 4
  hinged, 168
  padding, 121
Cassatt, Mary, 26
  monotype, 25

Castiglione, Giovanni Benedetto, 11–16
  monotypes, 12–16
  three methods used by, 12–16
Cauldwell, Leslie, 31
Cellocut, 57
Celluloid plates, 96
Chains, 99
Chang, Hsuan, 60
  rubbing, 66
Charcoal paper, 101
Chase, William M., 18, 21
Ciconi, I., 17
Citron, Minna, 87
  etchings, 150–152
City Art Museum of St. Louis, 31
Clay tile plates, 28
Coffin, Charles A., 21
Collotype, 57
Combs, 99
Coopman, Augustus, 31
Copper plates, 95, 99, 158, 167
Corot, 26
Cosimo, Piero di, 140
Cotton
  batting, 99, 102
  dabber, 111
  pads, 123
  swabs, 111
Cover papers, 101
Crayon, 96, 97, 101
  colored, 167, 179
  Korns, William, lithographic, 167
  monotypes, 162
Crepe paper, 142
Croce, Benedetto, 3
Crossgrove, Roger
  monotypes, 164, 165
Cutout shapes
  cardboard, 4, 154
  metal, 4, 154
  wood, 4
Cylinder transfer, 145, 153

Dahlgreen, Charles W.
  monotypes, 38, 39
Dali, Salvador, 142
  drawing, 124
David, Allen
  monotype, 71
Day, Worden, 87
  relief print, 148
  woodcut, 148
Degas, Edgar, 26, 28
  monotypes, 26–28
Dobkin, Alexander, 63
Drabkin, Stella, 57
  multitypes, 60, 61
Driers, 97, 142
  Japan, 99
Dubuffet, Jean, 47
  monotype-collàge, 49
  painting, 49
  painting-collàge, 48
Duveneck, Frank, 18
  monotype, 19
Dyes, 57, 96

Eaton, Charles Warren, 31
Eichenberg, Fritz, 63
  monotypes, 79
Electro-Monotype, 22, 23
Elmer's glue, 154
Elshin, Jacob, 87
Enamel
  drier in, 98
  synthetic, 97
Engraver's papers, 101
Ernst, Max, 42, 60, 142
  painting, 125
Etching, 3
  inks, 96, 97, 142
  monotype, 158
  papers, 101

Etching—(Continued)
  press, 99, 120, 154, 168
  Rembrandt's, 10, 11
  Venetian, studies, 161
Extender
  definition, 98
  in paint mixtures, 142
  silk screen paint, 97, 98
  starch, 175
  textile paint, 98

Fabrics as tools, 99
Fast drying
  inks, 120
  paints, 120
Fearing, Kelly
  paintings, 127
Ferrari, Giovanni Andrea de, 13
Fiberboard
  as pressure equalizer, 121
  panels, 97
  plates, 96, 102
Fingerpaint, 174
  paper, 101
Fitzsimmons, James, 50, 51, 57
  monoprint, 59
Flatiron, 168
Floatagraph, 59, 62
Florist's tissue, 101
Forain, 26
Foster, Enid, 59, 66
  monopens, 168, 169
Frasconi, Antonio, 87
Fresnaye, de la, 42
Freymann, 26
Frottages, 60

Galvanograph print, 23
Gauguin, Paul, 28
  manuscript, 31
  monotypes, 29–34
Gilchrist, 15
Glass plates, 3, 95, 102, 179
  ground, 162, 167
  milk-white, 107
Glue, 98
Glycerin, 98, 175
Goldstein, Milton, 59
  monoprint, 64
Gouache, 96, 174, 179
  binders, 98
  thinner, 98
Goyu paper, 60
Graves, Morris
  painting, 126
Gropper, William
  monotype, 88
Gum Arabic, 98

Hart, "Pop," 47
  monotypes, 51, 52
Hankins, Abraham, 66
Harrison, James, 57
Haskell, E., 31
Hayter, William Stanley, 59
Heat transference, 168
Herkomer, Sir Hubert von, 21, 22
  monotype, 24
Herkomergravure, Herkotype, 22
Higgins, Eugene, 31, 47
  monotypes, 40, 41
Hinge, masking tape, 120
Hoffman, Seth, 66
  monotypes, 86, 87, 104
Honey, 175
Howells handmade papers, 101
Hypo, 161

Illustration board, 101, 145
Importers, paper, 102
Inks
  blockprinting, 97
  etching, 96, 97
  lithography, 96, 142

Inks—(Continued)
  printing, 96, 97, 102, 142
  water base, 174, 179
Institute of Design, 42
Irvine, Wilson, 59
  floatagraph, 63

Jefferson, Joseph, 18
Johnson, Buffie, 57, 63
  monoprints, 83, 84

Kaar, Virginia, 63
Kahn, Max
  monotype, 89
Kerosene, 97, 102
Kirsch, Dwight, 66, 175
  monotypes, 158, 159
Kjargaard, John, 87
Klee, Paul, 42, 47
  paintings, 46, 47

Lahey, Richard, 87
  monotype, 88
Lasansky, Mauricio, 59
Lauber, Joseph, 18
Lautrec, 26
Lawson, Leslie
  monotype, 71
Leme, Bella, 63
  monotype, 74
Leonardo, 11, 140
Lepic, Count, 26
Letter press, 99
Linoleum
  block, 155
  plates, 96
Linseed oil, 98
  boiled, 98
  sun thickened, 99
Linweave Japan paper, 102
Lithography, lithographic
  crayon, 115, 167
  inks, 96, 142
  Korns, William, crayons, 167
  media, 179
  papers, 101
  trades, 125, 145
  zinc plates, 167
Loeb, Louis, 31

Machine oil, 98
McLaren, Robert, 87
  blockprint, 147
  blockprint-monotypes, 146
Margo, Boris, 57, 63
  painting, 133
Marxhausen, Benjamin
  student's can paintings, 141
Marxhausen, Reinhold, 153
Matisse, Henri, 42, 107
  monotypes, 44, 45
Maurer, Alfred, 47
  monotype, 55
Media
  crayon, 96, 97
  definition, 96
  dye, 96
  gouache, 96
  mixed, 8, 179
  oil, 96, 102
  poster paint, 97
  printers' ink, 96, 97, 102
  starch, 174
  tempera, 96
  watercolor, 96
Meo, Salvatore S., 63
Metal plates, 3, 95, 102, 158, 179
  heating, 123
Mielatz, C. F. W., 31
  photogravure of monotype by, 42
Miller, Charles, 17
Miller, Robert, 87
Minar, Earl
  monotypes, 131, 132

Mineral oil, 98
Mirko
  monotypes, 165–167
Mixed media, 8, 179
Modern Spirit and Catholicism, 31
  covers from, 32, 33
Monogouache, 57
Monopainting, 57
Monopen, 59
Monoprint, 57
Monotype
  a child of printmaking and
    painting, 5
  additive, 105, 115
  a means of creative invention, 8
  a planographic print form, 3
  a useful technique, 4
  Australian, 68–71
  blockprint, 155
  book, magazine, illustrations, 63
  definition, 3, 4
  etching, 158
  exhibitions of, 5
  in art instruction, 42, 65
  invention of, 13
  limitations of the, 5
  near, process, 154
  neglect of the, 5
  odd character of the, 5
  parties, 34
  photograph, 161
  second rate citizenship of the, 5
  single impression, 4
  sketches for painting and sculp-
    ture, 42
  subtle and beautiful effects of, 5
  subtractive, 105–107
  subtractive lineal, 107, 108
  subtractive tonal, 108
  true, 4, 26, 154
  watercolor, 174
Moran, Peter, 18
Moriki paper, 102
Morris, Carl
  painting, 126
Moy, Seong, 87
Mulberry paper, 102
Multiple
  duplication, 4, 5
  impression, 142
  printing, 145
Multitype, 57, 60, 61
Mulvey, Frank, 161
  nature photographs, 6, 7
  photo-monotype, 153
Murals, 87, 97, 155

Natsuma White paper, 102
Nasmyth, James, 21
Newman, Ernest, 87
Newspapers, 102
Nordhausen, Henry, 66

Offset process, 145
Oil, oils
  binders, 98
  driers added to, 99
  fast drying, 99
  paints, 96, 97, 106–108, 145, 179
  salad, 179
  slow drying, 5, 98
  stand, 107, 145
Oil cloth plates, 96, 142
Okawara paper, 102
Onionskin papers, 101
Osaka paper, 102
Overlay printing, overlays
  glazing, 142
  printing inks for, 99
  two or more, 4, 60, 61, 125, 132,
    142

Paggi, Giovanni Battista, 13
Paint
  artists', 97
  enamel, 97
  finger, 174
  house, 97

Paint—(*Continued*)
  oil, 96, 102
  poster, 97
  rags, 102
  silk-screen, 97
  tempera, 96
Painting
  brayer, 149
  easel, on paper, 155
  transfer, 149
Palette, 102
Paper, 101, 102
  absorbant, 125
  black, 172
  importers, 102
  photographic, 161
  preparing, for printing, 108, 111,
    113
  slick, 125
Paste, starch, 174
Pastel
  as mixed media, 179
  over monotype, 28, 164
Patecky, Albert, 66
Patterson, Ambrose, 87
  monotype, 92
Peixoto, E., 31
Pencil paper, 101
Pennell, Joseph, 158
Phenol, 175, 179
Photograph
  monotype, 161, 162
  print drier, 154
Picasso, 42
Pissarro, 26
Plastic plates, 96, 99, 102, 179
Plate Printing, 22
Plates
  celluloid, 96
  clay tile, 28
  copper, 95, 99
  fiberboard, 96
  glass, 3, 95, 102
  ground glass, 162, 167
  linoleum, 96
  maple, end grain, 172
  metal, 95, 102, 123, 179
  milk-white glass, 107
  oil cloth, 96, 142
  plastic, 96, 99, 102, 179
  sandpaper, 167
  without incised lines, 4
  wood, 96, 99
  zinc, 95, 99
Plats du jour, 28
Plywood, 121
Poppy oil, 98, 120
Portinari, Candido, 63
  monotype, 74
Powder, Carborundum, 167
Pozzatti, Rudy
  etching, 149
Prendergast, Maurice, 31, 47
  monotypes, 35
Presses, 99, 102
  blockprint, 99
  clothes wringer, 99, 120, 168
  etching, 99, 120, 154, 168
  letter, 99
  mechanical, 168
  spoon, 99, 102, 113, 168
Preston, Margaret, 63
  monotypes, 68, 69
Price, Vincent, 31
Printing
  ink driers, 99
  inks, 96, 97, 102, 106, 154
  overlay, 4, 60, 61, 125, 132, 142
  papers, 101, 102
  slow drying, inks, 5
  trades, 57, 125, 145
  water base, ink, 174
Prints
  drying of, 123
  galvanograph, 23
  multiple duplication of, 4, 5
  on transparent papers, 123
  photographic, 161

Prints—(*Continued*)
  second, 115, 122, 123
Prototype, 50, 58
Pugh, Clifton
  monotype, 70

Rasmusen, Bettie
  monotype, 117
Rasmusen, Henry (*author*)
  crepe print, 129
  main contribution, 123
  monopaintings, 176–178
  monotypes, 122, 136
  painting, 139
Recollections of a Picture Dealer, 28
Register marks, 120, 122
Rembrandt, 11, 13, 18
  etching, 10
Renoir, 26
Ret, Etienne
  monotype, 76
Retouching, 121, 122
Rhodes, Daniel
  monoprints, 172, 173
Rice papers, 101, 102
Rivacova, Leonica
  monotype, 75
Rivers, Walter
  painting, 175
Rohland, Paul
  monotypes, 118, 119, 145
Roller
  rubber, 99
  steel, 99, 113
Rouault, Georges, 42
  monotype, 43
Rubbings, 60
Rubens, 13
Ryan, Ann, 87

Salad oil, 179
Salkauskas, Henry
  monotype, 70
Sandham, Henry, 18
Sandpaper, 167
Sargent, John S., 18
Schanker, Louis, 87
Schleeter, Howard B., 66
  monoprints, 137, 138
Schoniger, 26
Schrag, Karl, 87
Second prints, 115, 122, 123
Shelf paper, 101
Shinn, Everett, 31
Shoji paper, 102
Silk screen
  extender base, 97, 98
  paints, 97
Sloan, John, 47
  monotypes, 50, 53
Slow drying oils, 98, 120
Smith, Charles, 50, 154
  blockpaintings, 57, 144
Society of Iconophiles, 34
Soyer, Moses, 31
  monotypes, 91
Spilimbergo, Lino Eneas, 63
  monotype, 72
Sponges, 99
Spongotype, 22
Spoon, 99, 102, 168
  table, 113
Stand oil, 107
Starch
  corn, 175
  extender-binder, 175
  laundry, 175
  medium, 175, 179
  paste, 174
Stencils, 142, 155
Sterne, Hedda, 63
  monotypes, 82
Sterner, Albert, 31
Sterner, Robert K., 66
Sticks, wooden, 99, 102, 111, 154, 172
Strathmore kid paper, 101
Stylus, 172

Subtractive
  lineal monotypes, 107, 108
  method, 105–107, 123
  tonal monotypes, 108

Tatham, 15
Tempera, 96, 179
Texture imprints, 50
Thick pigment technique, 115, 123,
  124
Thinners, 97, 98, 102
Thin pigment technique, 115, 123–
  125, 132, 140
Tin can painting, 153
Tissue paper, 101
Tolman, Ruel P., 31
  monotypes, 36, 37
Tongue depressors, 99
Tools, 99
  basic, 102
Toothbrushes, 99
Tourtelot, Madeline, 57, 66
  monogouaches, 160, 161
Tracing paper, 101
Transfer
  cylinder, 145, 153, 154
  drawings, 172
  heat, 168
  painting, 149
  techniques, 4
Transparent
  base, 60
  papers, 123
Treacy, Rea
  monotype, 112
Treatise on Painting, Leonardo's,
  140
Troy, Adrian, 87
True monotype, 4, 26, 154
Turner, Ross, 18
Turpentine, 97, 102, 145

Urruchua, Demetrio, 63
  monotypes, 73

Valadon, 26
Van Dyck, 13
Van Sloun, Frank, 66
  monotype, 56
Varnish, 98, 99, 107, 145
Vasari, 140
Vegetable oil, 98
Vollard, 28

Walker, Charles A., 21
  monotypes, 21–23
Walkowitz, Abraham, 47
  monotypes, 54
Watercolor, 96, 97
  monotype, 175
  opaque, 174
  paper, 101, 145
  pencil, 101
  transparent, 174
  tube, 179
Watkins, Franklin
  blockprint-monotype, 149
Wax paper, 120
West, Pennerton, 87
  monotypes, 90
Whistler, James McNeil, 18, 161
Wood, John
  monoprints, 170, 171
Woodblock
  medium, 179
  monoprint, 64
  transfer, 154
Wooden
  plates, 96, 99
  sticks, 99, 123, 154, 172
Wringer, clothes, 99, 120, 168

Yunkers, Adja, 63
  monotype, 78

Zebu paper, 102
Zinc plates, 95, 99, 167